SUSAN RAVEN, a singer-songwrit
British music festival scene, is a
Specialising in the Western esote
Rudolf Steiner, she regularly give:
elemental beings that inhabit it. Her   , ...u ner moving
and inspiring live performances, have attracted a large fan base
around the world.

Susan has spent the last 14 years living in the remote hills of mid-
Wales, deepening her understanding of the elemental kingdom and
gradually developing the faculty for perceiving this formative world
and its inhabitants. In her work she speaks openly of her transformative experiences, and has introduced spiritual-scientific concepts of the etheric world to many people over the years.

NATURE SPIRITS THE REMEMBRANCE

A GUIDE TO THE ELEMENTAL KINGDOM

SUSAN RAVEN

CLAIRVIEW

Clairview Books
Hillside House, The Square
Forest Row, East Sussex, RH18 5ES

www.clairviewbooks.com

Published by Clairview 2012

A catalogue record for this book is available from the British Library

ISBN 978 1 905570 37 9

Cover by Morgan Creative featuring photographs by Satch Norton
Typeset by DP Photosetting, Neath, West Glamorgan
Printed and bound by Gutenberg Press Ltd., Malta

MIX
Paper from
responsible sources
FSC   FSC® C022612
www.fsc.org

Contents

'When man begins to achieve peace within himself, his words grow stronger. They become more capable of encouraging and comforting his fellow human beings; they become effective among the elementals as well.'

'Much that seems today simply part of the order of nature, to be relied on as a matter of course, will before very long begin to fail, if men do not bring it to their active help, in return for all that they themselves have received.'[1]

Adam Bittleston

Introduction

Every human being shares a common goal. It is to understand and affect our experience of life while we are incarnated here on Earth. This endeavour is consciously and unconsciously driving us with nearly every breath we take. It drives us to assimilate and create our experiences in a multitude of different ways, and in my own case this journey of assimilation and creativity has expressed itself primarily through the media of song-writing and singing. Alongside my song-writing, I have also spent many years contemplating the mysteries and rhythms of nature, and searching a wide range of esoteric literature for answers to a question that has been with me for most of my life. It is not an unusual question, but one that many human beings have deliberated on over the millennia, one that resonates deep within the waking consciousness of many of us. It is quite simply this: 'What lives behind the physical, sense-perceptible world of nature and from whom did this great imagination of the natural world arise?'

(This question anticipates the existence and activity of the spiritual hierarchies. It also anticipates the existence of a living, imaginal world, and the influence this imaginal world has upon the physical world.)

I believe this question first began to arise in me at the age of eleven, when I visited the Temple of Apollo at Delphi during a family holiday to Greece. Not only is this sanctuary one of the most exquisite temple sites in the world, it is also the physical location of one of the most potent aphorisms ever given to humanity – the imperative to 'know thyself'. This famous directive is inscribed in the temple forecourt, and no better advice has ever been given to man or woman. Although I cannot consciously remember reading these words, I can trace the first beginnings of that now familiar inner turbulence which precipitates an artistic or spiritual endeavour to this time.

During my early, unsteady steps on the path of 'knowing thyself', I learnt that each one of us is born with a set of celestial coordinates, a starry script, which indicates the gifts and challenges we must meet in our present incarnation. I soon realized that one of my major challenges in this particular incarnation was the ability to communicate effectively with my fellow human beings. For many years, the highway from imagination and inspiration, to articulation and conversation, was littered with steep speed-bumps. Yet, these hindrances always yielded a gift at their higher octave. By working through them, I have learnt to combine authentic self-expression and emotive reportage in an art-form which utilizes what I have come to realize is one of my most useful gifts of this lifetime — my singing voice. In the writing and singing of a song, I have found that a personal, truthful disclosure can be crafted with insightful care, and given emotive and powerful impetus by the musical arrangements beneath it. The sounding of chords and tones has always offered us a sublime and powerful vocabulary with which to convey the language of an open heart; add to this a vibrant and reciprocal relationship with the intelligence in nature, and one can access a truly boundless source of inspiration.

For most people the business of communication is limited to the relationships we shape with our fellow humans and, to a lesser degree, the more utilitarian relationships we forge with the animal kingdom. To openly admit to an ongoing reciprocal relationship with the plant and mineral kingdom can be a daunting step, and can invite both derision and ridicule. However, we have reached a point in time where the need for direct communication with all four kingdoms of the Earth has become both urgent and essential to our survival as a species. In the following chapters we will be exploring how we can develop a conscious reciprocal relationship with the natural world around us.

I have the great good fortune to live in the remote hills of mid-Wales. The landscape here is alive with a potent and creative force, and the old clairvoyance our ancient ancestors once had — that great gift we lost when we took up full residence in the mind — seems only a glance and an in-breath away. The membrane between worlds is thin, and the nature spirits of the four elements are generous with their inspiration, but only to those who walk with love and mindfulness through their domain. It is easy to see how tales like *The Lord of the Rings* were born in this landscape; in one moment the land is a gateway to a sunny, gentle fairy realm, and in the next it is a fierce and towering presence that impels you to take account of who you are and what you ˏve done. Through my daily communication with the spirit of this land, I have begun to receive some answers to the enduring question posed above. Hidden meanings leap out and reveal themselves when I least expect them, but only after I have shown the necessary persistence and patience. My reaction to these responses is usually to laugh out loud, and afterwards to feel a strong sense of community with the living presence in the land!

The task of the troubadour has always been to listen to the wind and anticipate the future, to discern the fine nuances of a spiritual age and to play the dual roles of receiver and transmitter. My many years as a songwriter and performer have encouraged me to go ahead and petition the hidden spirit within nature to reveal its inspirations and imaginations. The song-smith and the emerging seer are mutually supportive. Yet we *all* have the ability to see into the supersensible world; it is not the province of a select few (if anyone intimates that it is, be very wary of the information they offer). In order to awaken this nascent ability within ourselves, we need to first acknowledge that we have the ability, then begin to awaken, develop and nurture it. Finally, we need to recognize its importance and relevance for our time.

Nature Spirits: The Remembrance is loosely divided into three parts. In the first part we investigate the new accelerated, evolutionary wave of consciousness pulsing into the Earth, and assess the effect it is having on orthodox views of science and history. We then take a look at the growing community of post-materialist scientists who are forging an undeniable link between science, consciousness and spirit, and explore the new ether science they are birthing into the mainstream. At the end of Chapter 1, there is an introduction to the philosopher and scientist Rudolf Steiner, whose spiritual-scientific views of the forces of nature have inspired forward-thinking scientists, artists and educators for over a hundred years.

In that section, we will also cover the following subjects:

(i)   a brief exploration of the vocabulary used to describe the activity of the quantum field and the supersensible world;
(ii) an investigation into the spiritual and scientific significance of the superwave phenomena emanating from the centre of our galaxy; and
(iii) a short overview of torsion field physics and the program-mable nature of DNA.

We learn how all physical substance can be described as an activity that has come to rest, or a divine thought that has slowed down, and in the dynamics of the ether we find the supersensible engine room where all the dissolving and coalescing forces behind physical matter exist. Each of these forces has a specific task in the moulding of matter in our sense-perceptible reality. Throughout our esoteric history these forces have been known as the nature spirits and elementals of the Earth.

For those of you approaching the subject of nature spirits and elementals for the first time, or for those of you testing this subject from a more orthodox and material understanding of nature, the vocabulary, imagery and examples used throughout the first third of the book seek to guide one through the ridicule and disbelief surrounding many aspects of the supersensible world today. The aim of this book is to awaken a spark of enquiry within, and to fire a new interest in the unseen forces working behind the visible, sense-perceptible world around us.

In the middle section of the book we trace humanity's path from the atavistic clairvoyance of our ancient ancestors to the modern, five-sense, intellectual interpretation of the natural world experienced by most people today. We then move on to a more detailed investigation of the nature spirits and elementals. We focus on the elementals of earth, water, air and fire, and take a close look at their activities in the world of plants. In this section we also contemplate the nature of the human body elemental, and take a look at the work of the fire spirits in human thinking. (I include my own personal experiences with the nature spirits of each element in this section.)

In the final section of the book we look at ways to prepare ourselves for a meeting with the elemental kingdom. Meditations and exercises aimed at developing the faculty of seership are offered at this point, with special emphasis on the importance of developing a relationship with the elementals in one's immediate environment. In the last chapter we look at the formidable healing power of forgiveness, and the effect it has upon ourselves and upon the Earth. We conclude by focusing on the vital need to become responsible co-creators at this critical time in our evolution.

There are many paths to seership extant in the world today, and the messages and directions offered here do not claim to be the *only way* to awaken this faculty. The contents of this book are offered in freedom, for you to explore at your own discretion and at your own pace. The path outlined includes a wide range of insightful testimony from some of the most experienced and well-respected seers working in the western tradition, both past and present. Their findings have been investigated and verified by many students of seership over the years.

If you are new to this subject, all that is asked of you is that you nurture an open mind and a willingness to contemplate an alternative world view. If the familiar sensation of doubt begins to intrude, simply witness that doubt and move it up to its higher octave of 'enquiry'. Then, if you choose to follow this path, with patience and practice you can reach an even higher level, which is a feeling of 'recognition' – a recognition and remembrance that tells you that you are contemplating a profound spiritual truth.

For those who wish to skip the scientific content at the beginning and go directly to the more detailed information on the elementals and nature spirits, I suggest starting the book at Chapter 3.

1

Bridge-building Between Science and Spirit

In this chapter we explore the following topics: the path of the scientist versus the path of the mystic; the emergence of a new ether physics and the scientists of a post-materialist age; the development of a modern path of seership, with an introduction to Rudolf Steiner and anthroposophy.

What lives behind the physical, sense-perceptible world of nature and from whom did this great imagination of the natural world arise?

There are countless sources of esoteric wisdom and material theories to explore and choose from in pursuit of an answer to this question. The answers streaming from our scientific institutions and universities show a formidable intellectual grip on the physical phenomena surrounding us. They are based on impressive, hard-won data and they give concrete physical meaning to much that had previously existed as theory and conjecture. The centuries of scholarly research and analysis have placed a scientific and mathematical structure of reference over the evolving world around us, and a consensual model of physical reality has been shaped by empirical data and years of replicable experimentation. To explore the mysteries of the universe and to anchor our findings in a temporal world, has ever been a consuming passion for humanity and, as with all quests, the real fulfilment lies in the journey itself.

This is also true for the path of the mystic, and it is the path of the awakening modern-day mystic we will be exploring in this book. Traditionally, the enlightened seers and initiates throughout history have always had a map and a language with which to penetrate aspects of the quantum physicist's world – a world where particles move backwards as well as forwards in time, where the universe is interconnected with instantaneous transfers of information, and where an observer's conscious attention affects the behaviour of subatomic particles. The dynamics of this unified quantum field would probably enkindle a spark of recognition in the eyes of an advanced spiritual seer of the past. He or she would see these dynamics as the gestures and expressions of spiritual beings working in the volatile dimensions between spirit and matter. Yet the shifting sands of time and the inexorable march of materialism have sculpted a new landscape over the old highways of initiation, and the traditional gifts and tools of seership have been lost to most of humanity. The esotericist's world view of evolution and the path of the initiate were either considered arcane and obsolete by materialists or subversive and dangerous by established religion; as the rise of intellectual reasoning and the ever-increasing pre-occupation with matter began to mould our modern-day consciousness, this occult knowledge retreated into closed societies where it was handed down from generation to generation or remained hidden behind monastery walls.

Today, however, the lid has been lifted; this previously hidden, or esoteric, knowledge is streaming out into the public domain and we are beginning to hear a more harmonious accord between leading spiritual thinkers of our time and certain members of the scientific community. A deeper understanding of the universal field of intelligence, which underlies and pervades us all, is drawing the two streams together and the gap is beginning to close. After years of outward separation, there are indications that science and spirit are at last beginning to show signs of fusing in certain areas, and for an increasing number of people in the scientific community attributing a spiritual, or supersensible, dimension to physical phenomena is no longer seen as a betrayal of ethics.

Some of the most high profile exponents of this new accord between science and spirit are the physicists Dr Amit Goswami, Dr William Tiller and Dr Brian O'Leary. They have chosen to venture into the domain of the supersensible in an attempt to interpret the seemingly inexplicable findings of their experiments, or to validate their intuitions about the existence of a spiritual world beyond physical matter and the quantum field. Dr Goswami spent over 30 years as Professor of Physics at the University of Oregon's Institute of Theoretical Science. He is a prolific writer, teacher and visionary and has appeared in the films *What the Bleep Do We Know!?*, *Dalai Lama Renaissance*, and the recently released, award-winning documentary *The Quantum Activist*. William Tiller is Professor of Science and Engineering at Stanford University, and is also founder of the William A. Tiller Foundation. His mission statement includes the following directive: 'To build a reliable bridge of understanding for nature's manifold expressions that (a) seamlessly joins with today's conventional scientific understanding of our outer space-time world, on one end, (b) passes through the various subtle domains of inner reality in the middle and (c) strongly joins with the domain of spirit on the other end.'[2] Brian O'Leary is a former astronaut and professor of astronomy at Cornell University, a co-founder of the International Association of New Science, and a clear and measured voice in the new consciousness revolution. He has spent many years exploring different modalities of spiritual thinking and practice, and has concluded, 'You can use the methods of science itself to verify and further develop metaphysical realities.'[3] His most recent book, *The Energy Solution Revolution*, which explores the reality, promise and ongoing suppression of clean and free energy research, directly addresses the socio-political and spiritual paradigm shift needed to implement global healing.

These are just three distinguished names on a growing list of 'post materialist' scientists who are emerging onto the world stage today – there are many more and the numbers are rising. William Tiller has stated repeatedly that humanity is going through a major consciousness transformation at this point in our history, and he believes that in many human beings a new brain is beginning to develop in reciprocal space.[4] This brain is seen as a higher organ of experiencing and knowing, able to assimilate both complex material theories and a multi-dimensional spirituality. It is developing in line with the individual's ability to consciously engage in enlightened, compassionate thinking, congruent moral behaviour and regular meditative practice, as well as his, or her, ability to thoroughly comprehend the physical sciences. Dr Tiller is joined by other high profile scientists and practitioners, propounding the existence of a newly emerging organ in reciprocal space. For example, the celebrated psychiatrist and author Dr David R. Hawkins has carried out many experiments using kinesiology to calibrate a person's level of consciousness, and to indicate the existence of what he calls the new 'etheric brain', or etheric extension beyond the cortex. In human history there have always been pulses of acceleration in the evolution of consciousness, and the potential emergence of a new etheric brain indicates that we are going through just such an evolutionary upgrade.

At the heart of the common core of mystical experience, recorded throughout the world's spiritual traditions, is the affirmation 'We are all one', and this deep truth is indeed being reflected in the field of quantum physics. What the mystic has always told us about the unity of all life, and what science is telling us about quantum coherency[5] and the non-locality of space and time, is sounding remarkably similar. However, to say that they are the *same thing* is to limit our view of Creation. Let us rather say that in this supersensible dimension the world organism is both a 'quantum superposition of coherent activities, with instantaneous, non-local, noiseless intercommunication throughout the system'[6] while also being a gateway to the 'peace that passeth all understanding'.[7]

There are of course those who eschew all spiritual and supersensible views of existence, and dismiss the common core of recorded mystical experience as mere speculation. The adherents of scientism, or conservative material science, uphold a purely scientific world view that encompasses natural explanations for all phenomena, and they consider nature's process of design as an inherent part of a self-organizing universe with no need of an interfering designer. Empiricism and reason are seen as the only appropriate tools with which to regulate reality and to comprehend the natural world around us. Matter is seen as the ground of all being and religion is considered an outmoded means of defining the *context* of the world we live in, while material science is seen as the ultimate instrument for defining its *content*.

Our European history shows us that the age of science and reason was born out of a fierce struggle with the superstitions of an all-powerful Church. The cardinals saw this emerging scientific view as a threat to their socio-political power and religious creed, and the Renaissance pioneers who gave birth to the new era of science were subjected to ridicule, intimidation and suppression. Maybe this battle still sounds on into the lecture rooms and laboratories of today, and maybe it continues to fire the denials of a supersensible reality so prevalent in certain traditional sections of the scientific community. However, if we gaze across the centuries, from the fifteenth century to the end of the twentieth century, we can see the arrow swing from one extreme tussle for power between science and religion to an altogether very different set of coordinates. Today, the tension is not about fundamentalist religion vehemently repressing a new stream of scientific knowledge; it is about a structured, established world order having to open up its borders and integrate a new multi-dimensional spirituality – one that seeks to transform *every* field of human endeavour.

The new renaissance wave we are riding today is far greater than the wave experienced in the Middle Ages; it is pulsing in from deepest space and sounding into the very structure of our DNA. We are a species at the end of an era, and our collective mind-dominated personality, which has sought to control everything with sense-based reason, is in the process of transformation, and a new multi-sensory human being is beginning to emerge. For those who are awake and aware, the task ahead is clear – to bridge the gap between the old and the new order with as much grace-inspired thinking, wise action and compassion as we can muster.

The path of material science has always focused on the evolution of life-form, and the esoteric path has always focused on the evolution of consciousness. However, as we advance into the new renaissance, the task of the modern-day mystic is increasingly concerned with the confluence of these two paths in our everyday lives. The pace of this integration will accelerate when a level playing field is established between science and spirit, and experiential knowledge of the divine, the discarnate and the supersensible is delivered in an intellectual and consensual way. These experiences cannot forever be dismissed as mere anomalies simply because science is unable to make an inventory of such things with its existing methods and models. When a truly multi-dimensional understanding of the nature of causation begins to direct our collective will, a new and heightened responsibility for everything we create will be impressed into the collective human consciousness.

By following a respected esoteric path or spiritual practice, a student can make advances beyond the sense-perceptible data of modern science and begin to experience the sensations of supersensible seership. This path usually commences with a detailed study of mystical experiences and observations recorded by the teachers, seers and mystics of a particular esoteric tradition. These records provide valuable points of orientation in the early stages of observance, and can indicate to the fledgling seer that he or she is experiencing an authentic vision and sensation. The path of enlightenment and seership has been documented in many traditions over the centuries. From Lao-tzu in sixth century BC China, to St Teresa of Avila in sixteenth-century Spain, to Sri Ramana Maharshi of Arunachala in twentieth-century India, to the esoteric streams of theosophy and anthroposophy in nineteenth- and twentieth-century Europe, the journey of enlightenment and seership follows a similar thread — a path of study, reflection, silence, purification, illumination and ultimately a profound union with all-that-is. It transcends individual religions and cultures, and it represents a universal truth available to all who are prepared to follow a specific set of mental, physical and moral coordinates into a dimension beyond the mechanics of mind, matter, space and time.

The path of enlightenment and seership has always been an arduous one and it calls for a relentless adherence to self-control. It involves regular meditation, contemplation and reflection, the recitation of mantras, and a firm commitment to compassionate and moral behaviour, both internally with our thoughts and feelings and externally with our words and deeds. The more attentive we become to our inner work, the more percipient and expanded our outward perception becomes. Then, in time, with a little patience and perseverance, this nascent seership begins to penetrate a world of formative forces, and at a later stage leads to a meeting with the organizing intelligence, or spiritual beings, who stand behind these forces. The rewards for this perseverance are life changing and, above all, life enhancing for both the individual and the whole of humanity. As this passage from the *Bhagavadgita* indicates, 'There is no purifier in this world to be compared to spiritual knowledge, and he who is perfected in devotion findeth spiritual knowledge *springing up spontaneously in himself in the progress of time*...'[8]

While it is true that only a few human beings ever reach a lasting state of union with all-that-is, each one of us can make a commitment to periods of study, silence and purification in our lives, and feel a real and tangible change for the better.

One of the most respected bodies of esoteric knowledge existing in the West today is the spiritual philosophy of anthroposophy, or spiritual science, brought to us by the philosopher and scientist Rudolf Steiner. A man of extraordinary and exceptional gifts, he not only possessed a clear understanding of all the material sciences, but he added to this a highly developed insight into the spiritual dimensions working within and beyond the physical matter of our sense-perceptible world. From an early age he was able to see clearly into a supersensible dimension which is closed to most of us. He developed his faculty of seership, or supersensory consciousness, to a level where he was able to enter this world in full waking consciousness and speak with precision about the relationship between spirit, ether and matter. His thorough grasp of the language and principles of material science enabled him to speak in exact terms about what he perceived in the supersensible world. In describing himself once, he said, 'No one will be able to say: this esotericist speaks of the spiritual world because he is ignorant of philosophical and scientific developments of our time.'[9]

Rudolf Steiner was able to present his views to the most hardened materialists and most discerning minds of his day with courage and confidence. He began to call his science of the spirit 'anthroposophy' in 1913, and the astonishing scope and vision of his work, which encompasses 30 books and 5000 lectures, is now available throughout the world. The Anthroposophical Society is secular; Rudolf Steiner wanted his work to be seen as a universal body of knowledge open to all, regardless of creed and nationality. In the later years of his life he was a man quietly and consciously harnessing supersensible forces for a formidable earthly task. And what was that task? To infuse the developed, materially driven western intellect with a new intuitive spirituality – a spirituality free from religious dogma.

He knew the time had come for humanity to develop a new conscious perception of the spiritual world, and he wanted to provide a link between the cognitive path of western philosophy, the sense-based data of science and the inner spiritual needs of the human being. Anthroposophy is not just another academic study, it is a transformational path of knowledge which has the power to change one's whole relationship to humanity and the natural world. A significant element in the early stages of this transformation is the level of *effort* one makes to truly understand the esoteric noesis[10] – merely reading the text is not sufficient. A practice of meditation, contemplation and digestion is essential in order to experience the real wisdom of this knowledge. By following such a practice, we can come to understand the enduring substance of our spiritual nature and see it emerging in every aspect of our daily lives.

Two of the cornerstone books of anthroposophy are *Occult Science* and *How to Know Higher Worlds*. The first title presents a history of evolution from a spiritually scientific point of view, and the second, self-explanatory title is Steiner's fundamental handbook for the modern-day spiritual pupil. The message contained in this handbook clearly shows us we all have the ability to develop our own cognitive awareness, and the sequence of instructions and exercises set out in the book have yielded successful results in aspiring students for many years. A budding spiritual scientist can measure and compare the authenticity of his or her experience with a large and varied body of previously documented accounts of the supersensible; and just as a material scientist's work is about testing a hypothesis and acquiring results through the verification of physical data, so the spiritual scientist's work is about the verification of internal spiritual experience and its subsequent effect on his or her understanding of the sense-perceptible world. The stabilizing questions on this often confusing and challenging path include: 'Is what I am experiencing real, and is it repeatable?'; 'Am I convinced by my own efforts and experiments?'; 'Do I truly believe in the results I am getting?; and 'Does my experience correlate with others following a similar discipline?' When the answer 'Yes' arises as a profound knowingness, the aspirant can then set a trajectory towards the higher stages of spiritual seership and illumination.

In the following pages we will be looking at the world of nature through the lens of spiritual science and learning about the spiritual beings who stand behind it.

2

Accepting a View into the Supersensible World: Tones, Torsion and the Cosmic Creative Word

In this chapter we view the following subjects: the influence of galactic superwaves on our planet and the programmable nature of DNA; the links between galactic phenomena, modern geological records and the symbolism of ancient mythology; torsion field physics and the cymatics of tone; transformative forces behind the accelerated changes taking place on Earth.

> 'All matter originates and exists only by virtue of a force which brings the particle of an atom to vibration and holds this most minute solar system of the atom together. We must assume behind this force the existence of a conscious and intelligent mind. This mind is the matrix of all matter.'[11]

> Max Planck

There are moments in life, often at times of crisis, when our personal world appears to stand still and we experience our whole history rise before us on a wave of emotion in the mind's eye. It is as though the evolutionary pressure within us surges upwards, carrying our entire biography with it. These moments are sometimes referred to as 'entering the gap'. They carry with them a precious opportunity to witness ourselves on the evolutionary ladder and an invitation to walk the path of spiritual enlightenment. Yet at such times many of us turn away from so piercing a revelation, preferring to reach for one of the many highly seductive and addictive sensory diversions available to us in the twenty-first century, hoping it will mask the restless unease. The struggle between the desire to be diverted and the impulse to evolve is a formidable one, but the relief provided by such transitory diversions can only be temporary, because our inner voice is destined to become ever more insistent until we acknowledge its message: that humanity and the earth are undergoing a period of profound change, and that each and every one of us has a unique opportunity to play a meaningful part in the unfolding transformation.

In order to understand and embrace the challenges of the future, we need to examine the past, and pay special attention to the cyclical nature of data and phenomena recorded in science, anthropology and ancient mythology. From the evidence embedded in ice-core readings to ancient prophesies proclaiming Earth changes and a split in humanity, to recent research showing how DNA is a programmable wave structure,[12] there is now a flood of information in the public domain — both speculative and proven — that points to the existence of a material and spiritual upheaval taking place on our planet. We are well into this challenging phase and the possible outcomes are many and varied.

One of the leading post-materialist scientists researching the cyclical phenomena recorded in geology, mythology, astronomy and astrology is the American astrophysicist and author Dr Paul LaViolette.[13] He presents a compelling body of evidence showing a correlation between major Earth changes and the arrival of galactic superwaves, or galactic bioenergy fields, in our solar system. Superwaves emanate from the centre of our galaxy and spiral out into space. They consist of cosmic electrons, gamma rays fired by super-charged particles, X-rays and gravity waves, and they travel towards our solar system at regular intervals with varying degrees of intensity. Dr LaViolette's data includes ice-core readings which measure the cyclical nature of cosmic ray intensity on the surface of the Earth, and it shows clear evidence of dramatic climate change at regular intervals, ranging from ice ages to severe drought caused by coronal mass ejections. The data also indicates that certain peaks, caused by a superwave entering our solar system, align with astrological cycles: for example the approximate 26,000-year cycle of the precession of the equinox and the 5700-year cycle of the Mayan calendar are marked by peaks in the data. According to Dr LaViolette, the Earth is due another substantial superwave in the near future.

There are also regular peaks appearing at much longer intervals, and they correspond to major upgrades in the complexity of life forms on the Earth. The work of Dr Robert Rohde, a physicist with a Ph.D from the University California, Berkley, shows how certain fossil records indicate a regular cycle of spontaneous evolution and the emergence of new life forms every 26 and 62 million years. This data appears to suggest that the biological upgrades on Earth coincide with a major superwave immersion. Mainstream biologists have named these jolts in the otherwise gradual pace of evolution 'punctuated equilibrium', and for those who firmly believe that behind every physical expression there is a spiritual impulse it becomes a logical step to assume that these giant spiralling waves carry with them a supersensible, spiritual directive as well as a physical one.

So what is the nature of the spiritual directive behind a spiralling superwave? And what is its relevance for humanity and the Earth? If we take into account the information left to us by the mystics of the past, and combine this with the emerging data presented by proponents of the new ether physics, and also include the theories of many leading spiritual thinkers of today, a possible answer may lie in the following statement: the new supersensible directive entering into earthly evolution at this time in our history is to upgrade and enhance all life on this planet, and, in the context of the human race, to augment a major shift in human consciousness by awakening dormant or 'junk' DNA within the human body. (DNA is a salt and a natural conductor of electricity. It is extremely sensitive to electromagnetic waves and as such would be responsive to the myriad kinetics of a galactic superwave.) So how is this done? In the language of ether physics, our DNA is absorbing a new coherent[14] light signature which is entering the Earth as part of a galactic evolutionary cycle. In the language of spiritual science, we are experiencing the effects of a new wave of elementals entering the etheric body of the Earth. The potentially positive effect of this new wave of light on each of us as individuals is dependent on our ability to connect with the higher, spiritual aspects of ourselves and our commitment to use the free will principle with wisdom and grace.

This spiralling, expanding growth principle applies to all levels of life in the universe. We can see evidence of the universal principle of spin, or torsion, unfolding throughout the kingdoms of nature, from the curve of a nautilus shell to the spiralling glyphs extant in ancient and indigenous cultures around the world. And now, with Dr LaViolette's research, we can begin to contemplate the macro scale spin of the galactic superwave as it pulses out from the centre of the galaxy, spins through the vast widths of space, and eventually passes through the physical and supersensible substance of our solar system and the Earth.

The creative deed of the spiral is also firmly embedded in the innovative theories of torsion field physics. This is a relatively recent field of scientific research which proposes that physical matter is indeed moulded by an ether of invisible, conscious energy. The scientific theory, observations and replicable experiments proposing the existence of this invisible, conscious ether emerged from one of the most talented and controversial thinkers of the twentieth century, the pre-eminent Russian astrophysicist Dr Nikolai Kozyrev (1908–83). He was not only considered a gifted and intuitive scientist, he was also known to have studied the path of seership. In his late twenties, his ability to access knowledge from the supersensible realms was considerably strengthened by a harsh turn of fate; he was arrested and incarcerated in a concentration camp for eleven years under the repressive laws of Josef Stalin. During this extreme and challenging period, Dr Kozyrev spent his time deeply musing the mysteries of the universe and honing his faculty of seership. In chapter one of *Divine Cosmos,* entitled 'The

Breakthroughs of Dr Kozyrev', by best selling author David Wilcock, he suggests that Kozyrev followed the spiritual path of preparation, illumination and initiation referred to in Rudolf Steiner's *Knowledge of the Higher Worlds and Its Attainment*. By following this path, Kozyrev was able to acquire a 'direct knowledge' of the ether, and a true understanding of the spiralling principles of time and torsion. 'From his illuminated observations, Kozyrev considered that all life-forms might be drawing off an unseen, spiralling source of energy, in addition to their normal properties of gaining energy through eating, drinking, breathing and photosynthesis ... the spiralling energy patterns in nature unveiled themselves to the initiated eyes of Dr Kozyrev ... and his "direct knowledge" informed him that this spiralling energy was in fact the true nature and manifestation of time.' He spent the rest of his life endeavouring to prove beyond any doubt that such an etheric energy had to exist.[15]

While it is beyond the scope of this book to give a comprehensive description of torsion field physics, the following elementary overview indicates how close we are to understanding the formative science behind some of the dramatic changes in species-evolution throughout our biological history. And on a more esoteric and philosophical level, it gives us a possible insight into the supersensible science working behind the spectacular deeds of creation enacted by the gods of mythology, as they boldly manipulated matter on an atomic and molecular scale. The old sagas and stories of the gods are the last relics of an ancient pre-religious consciousness. They represent fragments of a vibrant supersensible reality that was once experienced by the atavistic clairvoyance of early human beings, and they also hint at a time when the will of man could work directly upon the growth and shape of the surrounding environment. So, let us attempt to link the creative out-breath of the gods with the creative spiral of the torsion field.

Torsion fields, which are also known as spin fields or vector fields, are said to define the density and quality of physical matter.

They are the coherent effects of the spin of particles in space – or the quantum spin of empty space. But of course, space is *not* empty. Dr Kozyrev maintained that space is filled with invisible torsion waves which exist at varying degrees of concentration, and that the mass of a physical object can be altered as a result of an alteration to the torsion field. He maintained that torsion field interactions are transmitted through space like electromagnetic waves, but they transmit their formative information without transmitting energy, and they are able to propagate in the future as well as the past. He also proposed that torsion fields have an impact on gravity, and that they travel at well over the speed of light. He was able to ascertain these speeds by initially observing the physical light of a star and then observing the area where this light was likely to appear in the future. He was able to detect the signature of the real-time presence of the star in space-time with his specially designed telescope, which was fitted with time-flow detectors located at the focal point.[16] The following extract from an article by physicist Yuri V. Nachalov explains this point further: 'The registration of the true positions of different stars could be interpreted only as registration of star radiation that had velocities billions of times greater than the speed of light. N.A. Kozyrev also found that the detector registered an incoming signal when the telescope was directed at a position symmetrical to the visible position of a star relative to its true position. This fact was interpreted as a detection of the *future* positions of stars.'[17]

It is not surprising that many of today's enlightened scientists view torsion field physics as a synonym for universal consciousness. The creative, super-luminal, momentum of the torsion field can be viewed as universal consciousness in action!

Elements of this emerging scientific world view of creation have long existed in the mystery wisdom of the past. For example, the concept of a music of the spheres and the tones of the cosmic creative Word have always indicated the power of sound to mould the material world. Tones and torsion are close siblings in the dance of creation, and in the view of spiritual science the whole solar system passing before the celestial alignments of the zodiac is regarded as a vast musical instrument. The music from this instrument is precipitating an on-going and awe-inspiring deed of cymatics,[18] and it is forever demonstrating the inherent responsiveness of matter to sound. The following quotation from Rudolf Steiner draws a graceful picture of this great cosmic instrument in action. He asks us to imagine 'the sphere of the more stable fixed stars and behind this the moving planets ... when a moving planet passes by a constellation of fixed stars, not just one tone but a whole world of tone resounds. So the realm of the fixed star is a wonderful cosmic instrument and behind it are the gods of the planets who play upon this instrument of the zodiac.'[19] Later in the chapter we will be looking at how Rudolf Steiner defines the reverberations of the cosmic creative Word as the deeds and expressions of the nature spirits, elementals and spiritual hierarchies.

Time, tones, torsion and light are the messengers and journeymen bearing the 'will of creation' between the implicit and the explicit, the enfolded and the unfolded, and the supersensible and sensible universe. Proponents of torsion field physics suggest that the impact on a given environment caused by such an influential 'messenger' as the galactic superwave can stimulate the torsion fields, or the quantum spin of 'empty space', to intelligently reassemble molecules within a system into a new and more highly evolved life form – be that system a solar system, a weather system, a human being or a collection of amoebae. The vast unified source field, or living ether, from which all life emerges is seen to be creating life forms based on a design template, or prototype, and periodically the template itself is modified and upgraded. This inevitably leads to the question 'Who or what modifies the template?', and any attempt at an answer will surely lead to an animated and heated debate between science and religion and everything in between!

Students of spiritual science and the initiates of the past have always seen this unified source field as an evolving, dynamic universe of living spiritual beings. The extensive investigations into Earth's ancient memory, recorded by advanced initiates like Rudolf Steiner, have allowed us to comprehend a more holistic and far reaching version of evolution. By contemplating these records, we are able to look back over aeons of time and see how exalted beings, and their elemental helpers, have moulded the material substance of our planet. We are also able to learn how they have guided the prototype human being from the rarefied heights of spirit to the current, individualized, physical being of free will, which we find ourselves occupying today. Such world views rarely enter the lecture rooms and laboratories of our mainstream scientific institutions, and if they do, they are usually swiftly dismissed. However, it is worth noting that even some of our most high-profile university lecturers are prepared to *touch* on the idea of a Creator Designer these days, albeit with a tentative smile! Dr Andrea Sella from University College London intimated this on the BBC series *Secret Life of Chaos* when he said: 'A really clever designer would treat the universe as a giant simulation, where you set some initial condition and just let it spontaneously unfold in all its pattern and beauty.'[20]

The question of who or what is the prime mover behind the upgrade in human consciousness will always eventually lead us to infinity, but we can make an attempt at an answer if we mix the vocabulary of ether physics with the vocabulary of esoterics. When we consider our particular neighbourhood of the cosmos, a partial answer to the question posed above would have to be the central core of our galaxy. Some scientists believe this central core is a black hole, while others like Dr LaViolette define it as an immense Mother Star many times greater than our sun.

The Mother Star of the Milky Way sits in a vast well of gravity in a very materialized state, and extends her creative influence out towards the far periphery of the galaxy, to a point where photons begin to lose their energy and everything tends towards a more homogeneous state before reaching the peace of pralaya. In the language of mythology and esoterics, a Mother Star would be considered as the seat of an exalted Spiritual Being, or synarchy[21] of beings, who preside over the entire expanse of a galaxy. A directive of this great Being would be to birth a spiral of galactic energy, consciousness and matter out into all the countless solar systems of the Milky Way, in out-breaths of varying strength and intensity. A prime example of an historic, earthly representation of this exalted Being is the Egyptian goddess Nut, or Nuit, depicted as an over-arching female form covered in stars. She is also depicted as a half human, half bovine form with an urn on her head, and she pours the Milky Way out into the vast expanse of the cosmos.

The birthing and creation rate is, of course, greatest at the central core of the galaxy, and according to individual philosophic or scientific viewpoints, the galactic core can be seen as a giant torsion field generator, sending out spherical waves of 'universal consciousness in action', which in turn define the quality of ether and matter in their pathway, or it can be seen as the source of an intelligent, loving and sacrificial out-breath of the spiritual hierarchies. Alternatively, this out-breath can be described in more orthodox terms as the action of an astronomical giant, endlessly spewing out vast quantities of energy and matter into space, which inevitably impact our solar system on a regular basis and affect the biosphere and life-forms on Earth. However one chooses to view this deed of creation, its course is set; it continues to ripple out across space and time in regular waves, and it continues to send an evolutionary stimulus down the time-lines and pathways of life itself. Each and every one of us is affected by the supersensible and material substance of this out-breath, whether we are conscious of it or not, and every one of us faces the free-will choice of responding to this stimulus in an enlightened way or remaining behind in the course of evolution.

With the new, accelerated, evolutionary wave pulsing into the Earth at this time, the onus is on each of us to direct our will towards a path of responsible co-creation with the elemental kingdom. The celebrated historian and teacher of ancestral, land-oriented, spiritual paths R.J. Stewart emphasizes this in the following way: 'The overall expansion and acceleration occurs wherever it may find an outlet: thus it will pour into hi-tech greed and globalization if that is what we embrace, or it will pour into spiritual awareness, if that is what we embrace. As always with powerful transformative forces, the accelerated change is neutral, and it is up to us to decide how we embrace it, and to choose through what channels we allow it to move us, change us, and ultimately change our world.'[22]

The holy texts of Earth's great religions give abundant reference to the existence of Creator Beings. The avatars and teachers who taught the pure wisdom at the core of each faith all point to a Creator, or order of Creator Beings, who give of their own substance in order that matter and form may exist. In recent years a salutation has appeared in print which particularly mirrors the gesture of this birthing out-breath; the first lines of Neil Douglas-Klotz's translation of the Lord's Prayer from Aramaic to English run as follows:

O Birther! Father-Mother of the Cosmos,
Focus your light in us — make it useful:
Create your reign of unity now.

The maxim to 'make it useful' is, of course, one of the prime stimulants driving humanity to evolve, expand and create. Whether we choose to create only for the good-of-self or we choose to create for the good of humanity and the Earth is an indication of the evolutionary path we have chosen to take.

Whichever path of knowledge we choose to examine, whether it be contemporary scientific data, current esoteric literature or the prophesies of our ancient ancestors, it is clear that quantum leaps in evolution have occurred regularly in our planet's history. And all the signs are here to show we have entered another such leap. The old paradigm is disintegrating and our planet can no longer support a world order based on fear, coercion, greed and competition.

Only grace, cooperation and a true understanding of natural lore can heal the wounds inflicted by a relentless and ignorant mal-treatment of our eco-systems. Behind the many loud and passionate voices calling for purification and change, there are millions of people in silent revolt against the legislation that has allowed this environmental vandalism to occur. The breathtaking greed, self-interest and conceit of many world banks and corporations has endangered us all as a species. A profound yearning is growing among many to live more gracefully, to connect once more with the wisdom of nature, and to understand the rhythms of the cosmos and their effect upon us. Daniel Pinchbeck, the inspiring and best-selling author of *2012: The Return of Quetzalcoatl*, has this to say: 'An ever-growing segment of humanity is becoming conscious of the culture of domination that has degraded the biosphere, annihilated local cultures, and locked us in a prison of constricted awareness. As more and more of us realize this, we will unify our intention to undertake the difficult work of superseding it.'[24]

* * *

At the fulcrum between the new ether physics and spiritual science, both of which operate at the frontiers of science and consciousness, and the more rigid, empirical stance of scientism, which inevitably marks these explorations as pseudo-science, there is a powerful pulse of accelerated evolution sounding into the Earth. It is birthed through the mind of the galaxy itself, and it is influencing every movement within the system, causing an emerging universal wisdom to feed into our collective culture at a specific pace and at a specific time. This great pulse of evolution is exerted and applied by the powerful spiritual beings who endeavour to restrict, as well as advance, our human evolution.

The renowned physicist Arthur C Clarke once famously said, 'Any sufficiently advanced technology is indistinguishable from magic,'[25] and an increasing number of people are becoming aware of this. Those who are awake and aware know that as much effort is needed for the attainment of spiritual enlightenment as is needed for the collection of an impressive inventory of physical data. A requisite level of spiritual maturity in humanity is essential, in order that we may safely manage this impending 'magic' in a mature, collaborative and loving way. Powerful etheric technologies are waiting in the wings, but are we sufficiently prepared for the life-changing consequences and responsibilities they will surely bring?

Our task today is to enable new human systems to arise — systems that are rooted in fairness, social and environmental responsibility, and honourable governance. When the true power of human consciousness is understood, and it is exerted with grace and generosity instead of greed and conceit, the predatory, war-mongering programme we have been trapped in for thousands of years will eventually disintegrate, and the longed for gifts of world peace and free energy will become a present time reality. With the ending of the dark age of Kali Yuga at the end of the nineteenth century, Rudolf Steiner predicted an ascent from the maya of materialism and a profound phase of brotherly love for humanity. But this ascent can only be achieved if we chose to rework our sacred bond with the kingdoms of nature, and we choose to develop a connection with the higher, non-physical aspects of ourselves. He named this potential phase we are about to enter the Brotherhood of Philadelphia.

3

A View into the Ether and its Inhabitants

In this chapter we consider the following topics: the structure of the ether and the nature spirits and elementals who inhabit it; the creative will of the angelic hierarchies and the influence they exert throughout the astral-etheric body of the Earth.

'The salvation of science will come from a return to magic and enchantment.'

Graham Hancock, author of *Fingerprints of the Gods*[26]

Since mankind has travelled into space, we have seen images of the Earth in her entirety, and a recurring response to these glorious pictures of our planet is a sense of how delicate and fragile her atmosphere appears against the great, dark expanse of space. Beholding images of this shimmering, delicate life-mist hugging the globe has triggered an awakening sense of reverence and responsibility in humanity. Within the visible, calculable, substance of our biosphere there also exists an etheric or planetary life-body, radiating its life forces in all directions. It permeates the mineral, plant, animal and human kingdoms with its life-giving, life-organizing power. The word 'ether' means 'shine' in Greek and we can come to understand this etheric life-body as a living, shimmering space of potential which matter fills in countless shapes, colours and textures. The myriad forms in nature exist because these radiating forces are directed in their flow and bound into matter. So, what is the true substance of the etheric body? And what animates and organizes the physical forms of our world into a cohesive whole? The answer is clothed in a diverse range of vocabulary. In the language of the new ether physics, the ether is part of a unified source field, an invisible dimension of torsion and subquantum kinetics, which is imminent, emergent and in a constant state of flux. In the language of the mystics and the modern seers of today, the ether is a great chorus of creator powers, nature spirits and elemental beings ... who also exist in a constant state of flux, who also initiate and propel the emergence of life, and who also exist in a continuous deed of creation.

The nature spirits, or elementals and devas as they are also known, are everywhere about us. They are the animating force behind the processes of nature, and without them our world would collapse. Although our eyes may not see them, they reveal themselves to us through their activities. From feldspar to apple blossom, from mountain mist to red hot lava, each seemingly inanimate object and each living organism has integrated and responded to these forces in a distinct and unique way. We can begin to understand these forces, and the nature spirits who are the carriers of these forces, if we carefully observe their *effects* on the natural world.

In order to enter the world of the nature spirits and to understand their work, it is essential to see the earth as an ensouled and conscious Being, and the nature spirits as her building and maintenance team. We are familiar with the sensations of the physical world through our five regularly used senses, but few of us are consciously aware of the etheric body surrounding our planet and the part it plays in our life. The etheric or life body of the Earth is where the formative, animating forces exist; it is where the living cooperation of a great plurality of elemental beings works into the physical substance and strata of the Earth, as an organizing and life-giving principle.

If we penetrate further, beyond the vibratory field of the etheric body and its elemental beings, we find yet another field of existence known as the astral body, or Devachan as it is called in the East. The astral body is where all the instincts and impulses, the sympathies and antipathies, and the feelings and memories of the world and its inhabitants reside. Every feeling, desire and emotion has an independent existence within this field and can be seen as a separate entity with its own vibratory signature. The astral body is the collective emotion of the planet, and while reductive material thinking may affect this field it has no official vocabulary to really explain it. It is a place where the primal cause of an impulse or disturbance meets a supersensible waveform and its sensible particle. It is where all the prognostics gather in a hovering field of potential and prepare to collapse into a present-time physical reality. The location of this supersensible body of the Earth is both local and multi-dimensional and, in essence, it is the soul of the Earth.

There are many worlds, dimensions and sheaths of existence woven into the fabric of our planet, and the soul or sentience of the Earth is the most sensitive and aware dimension of our world. For many people the name of the soul of the Earth is Gaia, and she is considered an offspring of the overarching sentience of the Milky Way.

Our galaxy is a vast primordial intelligence, an exalted personality within the whole of creation, and our solar system has its own personality, intelligence and sentience too. In this gigantic galactic super-organism, the background quantum energy source field from which all matter is born exists at different densities and different levels of consciousness. Through the lens of spiritual science, and in the esoteric records of many spiritual traditions, these varying states of consciousness, or 'layers of God', are perceived as angelic hierarchies. From each level, the elementals on Earth are being directed in a specific creative task by a synarchy of advanced creator beings, or an order of the spiritual hierarchy. There is a natural organizing of responsibilities within the whole system and each entity is engaged in an interactive dance of mutual reciprocity throughout an evolving, dynamic field of living spiritual beings.

If we observe the titles held by the great creator beings in the Judaeo-Christian esoteric tradition, we can discover names like the Elohim and the Thrones. However, in his fundamental work *Occult Science*, Rudolf Steiner chose to add a new set of titles to the traditional names of the spiritual hierarchies. These new titles indicate the creative responsibilities of each level of the hierarchy, and point to their specific task in the evolutionary development of mankind and the formation of the Earth. For example, the hierarchy of the Elohim or Exusiai, who are described as the artisans of the solar system, have been given the title Spirits of Form; and the hierarchy of the Thrones, who are described as putting the 'mind of God' into practice, have been given the title Spirits of Will.

For the past 500 years, the plurality of the Creator has been neglected in the West. In the sphere of religion God has become a sole creator, and in the fields of science and intellectual reasoning the idea of a spiritual hierarchy interweaving the world of our five senses would be regarded as an archaic, esoteric musing. Yet, the overriding message sounding in from these exulted spiritual beings, as recorded in spiritual science and many other esoteric traditions, is their desire to see humanity return from its isolation and abandonment of the spiritual world, and to fulfil its destiny as responsible, conscious co-creators of the world. An increasing number of people are receiving this message and are waking up from the collective amnesia that has held sway for so long.

Before our planet became the solid sphere we know today, it underwent a long process of densification over aeons of time. If we look through the lens of spiritual science, we can learn how the Earth came forth from the twilight of a great nebula — a nebula inhabited by a whole choir of spiritual beings. Matter can do nothing unless spiritual beings inhabit it and consciousness is behind it, therefore this great choir of advanced creator beings proceeded to order and mould the substance of our solar system into the form it takes today. Alternatively, if we are to use the language of ether physics, we could say that these beings initiated the spin of the torsion fields and precipitated the unfolding of the time-space continuum. Throughout history, the creator beings have been anthropomorphized in countless ways and they have had many names over the ages. They stand in powerful majesty behind all the major shamanic and esoteric traditions around the world. They are interconnected through countless fields of existence and they are part of a vast, primordial intelligence, thrumming throughout the universe. They receive and emit an endless song of creation, which the elementals on earth then implement into the apparently solid, time-space reality in which we live.

Our creation myths appear to be almost holographic. All over the Earth, the same core message seems to underlie each individual folk lineage, and the recurring theme running through these ancient myths and legends is one where the gods sacrifice a part of their own being in order that a living, primal substance may come forth for the creation of a sense-perceptible world. This sacrificial, primal substance then undergoes countless transformations, condensations and rarefactions before emerging as the tangible, living world we recognize today. By this deed of sacrifice, the hierarchies of creator beings further their own divine evolution.

The physical substance of our planet and the myriad life forms existing upon it have undergone a magnificent process of moulding over aeons of time. So, the next time you hold a pebble of granite in the palm of your hand and admire the veins of glittering quartz running through it, or you take some time to contemplate the human hand itself, remember that through countless ages exalted spiritual beings have sounded through space and time, and worked into matter to bring these magnificent forms into a vital and solid state.

As the sphere of life and the nature kingdoms within it became more physically manifest on Earth, the creator powers withdrew from the denser spheres and retreated to higher spiritual regions, or higher Devachan, where they are able to work into the Earth from the periphery. They delegated the business of rotation, rhythm and physical matter to less advanced angelic and elemental beings, who are better constituted to work in a more dense environment. The creation of elemental beings came about through a sacrificial separation, or a tying off of parts, from the creator powers. These detachments then emerged as newly created groups of elementals, which developed over time to become the indispensable helpers of the higher hierarchies. They are continually being sent into the world to be enchanted or bound into matter and, while in this enchanted state, they organize, animate and delineate space for the billions of diverse physical forms on our planet.

The elementals on Earth have no free will or moral responsibility at this current phase of their evolution. Their consciousness is matter itself. They are programmed to participate in creation and must undergo countless enchantments and releases from matter, until they are deemed ready to advance. In their field of ceaseless movement and endless becoming, they carry out the instructions embedded in what will be described as the 'cosmic Word'. As it rings through space and time, and sounds into the layers of the Earth, it brings order and measure to physical form and it sets limits to matter. It is the universal song forever singing its 'self' into being, and Rudolf Steiner explains this process exactly when, in his lectures on agriculture, he says: 'What the elemental beings have called into the world is the last reverberation of the creative, formative cosmic Word, which underlies all activity and all existence.'

Quite simply, without the elementals there would be no solid Earth.

This profound knowledge of the formative forces animating our physical world is absent from most curricula in schools and universities today. For years, mainstream education has taught a purely intellectual, sense-perceptible view of the world, where only material criteria are deemed worthy of consideration. This approach has fulfilled a necessary chapter in the evolution of human consciousness, and later we will be considering the esoteric reasons why this is so. However, today we have reached a turning point. It is now time to awaken and develop our dormant faculties of perception to the point where we are able to observe and understand the deep laws of life emanating from the supersensible world. One of the most important objectives to achieve in the present age is the ability to directly experience this living, etheric field of information and to recognize its patterns. The quality and movement of the ether determines the surface outline and character of physical matter, and as sentient beings with free will we have the potential to enhance the quality of both ether and matter with our forces of thinking, feeling and will.

The inspiring viticulturist and author on biodynamics[27] Nicolas Joly explains the interaction between ether and matter precisely when he says, 'Matter does not create forms, it harmoniously fills the contours organized by the action of intangible forces.'[28] So, what are these intangible forces? Are they random, arbitrary forces emanating from a soulless universe? Are they a self-organizing principle that just happens to be there? Or do they emanate from a great synarchy of creator beings and elementals, who animate and organize physical phenomena in a precise and measured way while simultaneously responding to feedback on the front line of an ever-evolving environment?

Complex and unpredictable as the algorithms in nature may appear, we will see a time of spiritual and moral maturity unfolding in the future, which will allow us a clearer view into the vast wisdom behind these formulae. We will then take our predestined place beside the hierarchies, as wise, conscious co-creators of our environment. This can only take place, however, if we evolve away from the destructive, fear-based, scarcity-consciousness perpetuated by oppressive corporate policy, immoral banking practices and politically manipulated media coverage of environmental events.

Expanding on the theme of responsible co-creation, Rudolf Steiner emphasized on many occasions that we need to treat the laboratory table as we would treat an altar. He maintained that a spiritual science must be placed alongside the physical, sense-perceptible sciences, and that we must take this science of the spirit absolutely seriously. To understand the deep laws of life from a spiritually scientific point of view must now become a prerequisite before we blindly unleash new technologies into our environment and precipitate further damage. Dr Steiner's clarion call does not reject the years of meticulous observation, the disciplined methodology, the passionate pursuit of answers or the tireless collection of scientific, sense-perceptible data carried out over the centuries, because such efforts have been an essential step on our evolutionary path. The impulse to investigate lies at the heart of the human free-will principle, and the rays of brilliance shown by so many members of our scientific community are a testament to the power of that free-will investigative principle. However, it is a supersensible knowledge that needs to permeate the scientific curricula of today. Exercises like calculating the atomic weight of elements and observing how they react to each other have been an essential classroom staple, but behind these physical connections and equations live elemental spiritual beings and a vast supersensible world history reverberating down into the processes.

The deep laws of life and the elemental nature spirits who direct and carry them out belong to a world just as real as the material world. It is now time to speak a new language with a vibrant vocabulary that conveys a true understanding of this domain of the vital forces. There is a new wave of spirituality sounding into the Earth, and it seeks entry to all areas of human activity. It is behind an accelerating evolutionary push, which is propelling us towards a more multi-dimensional way of being. If we open up to this wave and allow it to awaken our dormant faculties of supersensible perception and cognition, we will begin to see the elementals and nature spirits at work, and to observe the spiritual laws governing life.

4

The Descent and Ascent of Consciousness

In this chapter we explore the following topics: the potential effects of the new ether physics on an awakening society; past civilizations and the development of human consciousness; the human birthright of seership and our potential bond of kinship with the elemental kingdom.

'Entirely new vistas open up when a widely accepted assumption is taken as the beginning of an enquiry, rather than as an unquestionable truth... The sciences are being held back by assumptions that have hardened into taboos. I believe that the sciences will be regenerated when they are set free. They will be more interesting and more fun.'[29]

Rupert Sheldrake

As we journey through the coming decades of the twenty-first century, we will begin to see the links between matter, ether and spirit become increasingly self-evident. If the momentum of change heralded by the new community of post-materialist scientists begins to grow and flourish unhindered, the old threats of ridicule and derision will no longer have the power to deter young scientists from taking a scholarly interest in humanity's occult history, or from examining the spiritual science behind many material theories and experiments. A new atmosphere of openness will begin to unfold. Instead of a fiercely competitive and often secretive system of research and development, a more honest and free exchange of information and a fairer, more enlightened distribution of funds will begin to be implemented. The relationship between consciousness, human thought and the activity of the elementals in the astral-etheric source field will also become self-evident. A new global bank of knowledge and an interactive system of disciplines, including the wisdom of spiritual science, will begin to work for the good of everyone instead of the profit of a few, and we will begin to rework the bond of life with other species and other dimensions of existence on our planet.

This viewpoint is not born out of an impractical and idealised vision of the future, but out of the need for an efficient use of Earth's precious resources, and ultimately for the survival of our species. The giant economic disparity prevalent today, with its attendant level of social and environmental injustice, is unsustainable. We have reached a point on our journey where the survival of humanity on the Earth can only be assured by the collaborative efforts of everyone — everyone, that is, who resists the downward, ever-hardening path of materialism, and chooses instead the upward path of enlightenment.

We will also come to see enlightened and innovative scientists like Amit Goswami, William Tiller and Paul LaViolette in the field of physics, and Rupert Sheldrake and Bruce Lipton in the field of biology — to name but a few — as the light-bearers of a generation. Their dynamic thinking, inner conviction and spiritual experience have opened the doors to a multi-dimensional version of science, a version that reintroduces a vital and much needed supersensible-etheric view of reality and consciousness. These innovative pioneers of the emerging post-materialist scientific era are mending a crucial bridge through time, and if we look back over this newly repaired bridge we will be able to discern a luminous trail of knowledge left by the light-bearers of the past. This flickering trail of light, flashed forth by the great avatars, seers and wisdom-keepers of the past, is becoming more obvious and relevant to people today as more of us become aware of humanity's esoteric lineage and the new light it sheds on established versions of human history.

When we become aware of our true lineage as spiritual beings undergoing a human experience, and we see how the Earth and its inhabitants have been the focus of a fierce struggle between the forces of greed and deception and the forces of freedom and enlightenment, more of us will find the courage to break out of the old fear-based model of reality and choose to become fully-fledged participants in the emerging transformational process taking place on Earth. In the decades to come Rudolf Steiner will be increasingly recognized as one of the most significant light-bearers of the nineteenth and twentieth centuries. His thorough investigations into the spiritual lineage of the human being and his detailed accounts of the astral-etheric realms provide a fountain of supersensible knowledge for the newly emerging community of post-materialist science. In his remarkable lectures on the structure of the ether and the beings who inhabit it, entitled *Harmony of the Creative Word*,[30] he gives an account of a very similar domain to the newly unfolding landscape of sub-quantum kinetics, gravitons, etherons and morphogenetic fields described in the new ether sciences. However, anthroposophy can take us further; Steiner leads us into the mind of the spiritual hierarchies, and into the living, conscious layers of creation. These lectures are accurate testimonies of the 'ether-in-action', and in the next chapter we will be taking a closer look at the similarities between anthroposophy and the etheric landscape of the new post-materialist ether sciences.

The language used to describe the two streams of science and spirit is often very different, but it is frequently describing the same phenomena. For instance, in a laboratory one would speak in terms of bio-photon emissions emanating from the cells of all living things, while in a class of spiritual science one would speak in terms of physical form being moulded and animated by the enchantment of elementals into earthly matter. Contemporary physics tells us that behind all form there is a supercharged backdrop, an energy exchange between supercharged particles. This backdrop, or field of formative forces, has been described by initiates in many ways over the ages as the presence and deeds of spiritual beings and nature spirits. The spiritual laws and beings governing this field were received and observed with clairvoyant vision by initiates in the ancient mystery centres of the world. Although the true clarity of the ancient visions and revelations perceived by the mystics of those far-off times has long since receded into the distant past, some semblance of the pure wisdom they received and imparted to their communities remains in the myths and legends that have come down to us in the form of folk and fairy tales.

However, a more direct knowledge of the wisdom taught in these great mystery centres was carefully safeguarded and preserved by initiates through the ages, despite cataclysmic social and environmental upheaval. Esoteric societies and shamanic lineages were formed all over the world in order to hold and protect this mystery wisdom. In some it remained pure, while in others it became distorted and decadent. Even up until the height of the Renaissance, spiritual scientists, or alchemists, prepared themselves with appropriate initiation training to experience the enchantment and release of spiritual beings in connection with changes in matter. However, the ability to do this became increasingly difficult, because humanity's innate clairvoyant faculties had almost completely disappeared by then. These faculties were being replaced by a growing impulse to experiment and control so-called inanimate forces with reason and intellect.

For humanity, the progression from a dreamlike consciousness under group-soul, or tribal, conditions to a full awareness of self as an individual has taken place over many epochs. It is analogous to the developing child, commencing life in a sleeping dream-state, rising through puberty and finally emerging into a fully-fledged, self-determining adult.

The leaders of humanity in early times were drawn from a priestly caste, and were deeply versed in the mysteries of nature's lore and the divine origin of the human being. This sacred knowledge was taught in the great mystery centres of early civilization and was handed down from generation to generation. While it is true that the Babylonian mysteries, the Egyptian and Hellenic mysteries, Gnosticism and Hermeticism, and the path of the Hebrew Cabbala, are generally considered to be the oldest mystery streams in our western civilization, each of these traditions was born out of a still more ancient stream that has long since receded into the mists of time. The physical evidence supporting the spiritual practice of these earlier civilizations is scant, but from general inference, coded mythology and the spiritual testimony offered by advanced initiates like Rudolf Steiner, who are able to access and investigate the Earth's history held in the Akashic Record,[31] we can trace the way of the great wisdom-bearers of the past. The springs and wells of universal, primal wisdom still flowed into the world in a pure form in the mystery centres of antiquity, and their locations were chosen to harness the telluric power of the Earth and the energy grids of the planet.

To stand in the presence of the massive stones of Avebury on winter solstice morn or to contemplate the stellar map of the pyramids on the Giza plateau is to stand in a vital presence of world memory. The fragments of meaning and memory are so tantalizingly close. They ignite a wish to remember our long-lost human history, and to sweep aside the curtain of forgetfulness and false information which has endeavoured to hide the truth of our spiritual and stellar origins for so long.

According to Rudolf Steiner's investigations, the teachers, leaders and initiates of these ancient times were carefully prepared to receive direct revelation from the spiritual beings responsible for humanity's evolution. They then orientated their people according to the revelations they received. Human beings in those remote times were constituted in such a way that they could receive a supersensible transference of knowledge and guidance directly into their open consciousness. This early supersensory constitution also allowed them to perceive and commune with the elemental beings in nature and to feel themselves completely connected to the soul of the Earth, and indeed, to the whole of the cosmos. We have acquired our modern consciousness at the cost of losing this direct, divine knowingness and the profound sense of belonging that goes with it. All the great world myths and legends point to a time when humanity walked with the gods, a time when the veil between the sense and supersensible worlds had not yet been drawn.

However, over the millennia, these old powers of supersensory vision began to fade, and the spiritual leaders in later civilizations could only make contact with the supersensible world through increased effort and discipline. The new path to knowledge was no longer via divine revelation, but through the power of thought directed to a systematic study of the natural world. Humanity's dreamlike state slowly gave way to a fuller, more complete incarnation into the world and a greater awareness of self. There was a closing off from the spirit world and humanity began to develop the faculties of thinking and reason. This evolutionary pulse sounded into our emerging western civilization with the birth of philosophy in Greece. The faculties of thinking, reasoning and logic began to replace the almost total reliance on divine guidance which had prevailed in the past. And in Greek sculpture, architecture and drama, humanity began to imprint a clear image of itself into the material world. This creative out-breath was a definitive step towards a self-reflective human being, preparing itself for individual free will. Seen through a certain lens, the spiritual hierarchies were letting their earth children go, step by step, in order that we might reason and think our own way through the world of form.

Then, as western civilization entered the era of Rome, humanity's developing faculty of thinking was increasingly drawn into ambitious deeds of civic engineering and a new rule of law. In the old forms of law, represented by the Law-book of Hammurabi, we can see that man's nascent individual personality was fused into a tribal whole, or folk soul, and fixed into a theocracy. In the Roman era we meet the concept of the individual citizen and an emerging structure of *man*-made jurisprudence. It is also during this period that we see a progressive transformation of Earth's resources into human wrought work. This evolutionary current was harnessed by an increasingly dominant, male authority, which began to completely overshadow the previously predominant, female, intuitive interaction with nature and the elemental kingdom. From the beginning of our own cultural epoch in the fifteenth century through to the end of the twentieth century, material science, mechanical law and the supremacy of matter have held sway. Our intellectual faculties and individual objective consciousness have developed in line with our descent into matter.

Over the past millennia, not only have there been great strides in science, architecture and art, but humanity's hunger for exploration, world trade and empire building has truly revealed the extent and power of our newly embodied ego-consciousness. Individualism and the growing sense of 'I am' inevitably sent shock waves through the old structures of governance, religion and tribal allegiance, but it also set in motion a great age of cultural and technical achievement. The ancient clairvoyance we once had as a natural, inborn gift has faded away; we appear to have won our independence from the spiritual hierarchies, and human free will has been truly unleashed into the world.

Yet this highly developed materialism and independent thinking has not delivered the promised freedom and utopia – it has instead brought us close to self-destruction. Today, a turning point has been reached; it is time for our precious but voracious intellect to be shot through with a new vein of brilliance based on profound spiritual insight and experience. From the heights of spirit to the depths of matter, our consciousness has descended the long stairway from heaven. In evolutionary terms, it has reached a point where its descent into matter is complete and it has almost forgotten itself. But for those who are awake and aware, the new wave of heightened consciousness raining into our mental world will begin to pivot our evolving intellect into a new direction. We will be graced with a new supersensory vision beyond the logical mind. We will pick up from where we left off in ages past and engage once more with the divine creative order and its elemental helpers. But this time we will consciously re-enter and negotiate the supersensible worlds in full waking consciousness, equipped with a self-directed, hard-won intelligence and the ability to reason for ourselves.

One of the most pressing assignments facing our newly awakening consciousness is the healing of our environment. We must learn to read in the great book of nature once again. The nature spirits are waiting to be reunited with us, and as emissaries of higher spiritual beings they wish to be of great assistance to us at this time. But we have to step into their world and meet them in their own territory. It is time to engage in dialogue and relearn a living world wisdom from the elemental kingdom.

Our developing intellect has done its best to ridicule and obliterate them, but a universal spiritual truth cannot be indefinitely repressed. Traditions and customs honouring the nature spirits exist all over the world and many of the younger generations are reviving old ceremonies and customs dedicated to the elementals. This is being done not just to preserve a quaint and charming folklore for posterity; it is being done to re-examine the supersensible laws underlying the structure and nature of these ancient customs.

The devastating path of transnational, corporate capitalism and rampant materialism has done its best to obliterate these reverential customs, but the indigenous peoples of the world have long accepted the responsibility of communing with the elemental kingdom. Their sacred ceremonies, which honour all elemental life, have been carefully passed down through the generations, and in remote, rural communities all around the world a regular offering to the nature spirits is seen as a necessary part of the daily routine. The aboriginal people of this planet have never lost their connection with the nature spirits; they have kept in place the bonds of kinship with these beings, and the preservation of this bond has been for the ultimate benefit of us all. In Iceland, knowledge of the 'Hidden Ones' is shared by many of the island's people, and the government even allows for an official recognition of nature spirits. As a result, many sacred places, known to be special areas of spiritual phenomenon, are protected. There is an innate, ancient, ancestral knowingness behind such offerings and protection. The world of form is seen as a conscious living whole, in which nature spirits and human beings are in constant interaction with each other. The pace of environmental decay could be considerably lessened if only we would accept the existence of these beings and work in harmonious collaboration with them.

Within today's consensual view of the thinking, feeling, biological human, there lies a misunderstanding or, in some cases, a deliberate cloaking of our true nature and hidden faculties. The innate ability of the human being to perceive beyond the physical world is dormant in most people today. But just as a laboratory technician aligns the fine focus adjuster of a microscope to explore the minute building blocks of creation, so spiritual science and many other respected paths of seership can teach the human being to develop a fine focus adjuster of his or her own. This faculty is an inbuilt cognitive ability and it is the birthright of us all. Anyone who chooses to make a commitment to the requisite meditative and spiritual practices can in the course of time become familiar with the laws and motions of the ether. It is simply a matter of choosing to make these required commitments, and using the intelligent mechanism of the entire body, especially the heart, to engage with the environment. If we choose to work only within the confines of the head we are living a partial version of who we really are, and by doing so we ignore a vital instrument within the human sensory tool kit. This potential instrument of cognition is hard-wired into every human being incarnated on Earth; it is time to acknowledge it, hone it and use it in service to all life on this planet.

As university tuition fees around the world hit record levels, it is time for the up-and-coming young students of the emerging new era to wield their formidable buying power and demand a more multi-dimensional version of science and history. This leverage could be used to ensure that a more enlightened version of human evolution be taught, before a new generation of graduates take on the life-changing levels of debt required for the acquisition of a university education.

The narrow bandwidth of sensory perception we have been operating in for the last 200 years will no longer serve us in the coming times of change, and awareness is the first step towards implementing that change. So without further delay, let us examine in detail the nature spirits and elementals of the four basic elements of earth, water, air and fire.

5

Gnomes, Undines, Sylphs and Salamanders

In this chapter we explore the following subjects: the nature spirits and elementals of earth, water, air and fire, and their activities in the world of plants; the nature of the human body elemental, and the work of the fire spirits in human thinking.

'The space is what defines matter, not matter defining the space. All matter emerges from the vacuum and returns to the vacuum, and once we understand this we lose our sense of separation... When the masters speak of their moment of illumination, they typically describe it as a unity with all things.'[32]

Nassim Haramein, physicist

We will begin our investigation into the supersensible world of the elementals with two questions and two definitions.

The first question is, 'What is an elemental?' An elemental is a nexus of subtly primed consciousness and vitality working at the junction between spirit and matter. It is a constituent part of an ever-evolving, life-giving expression of divine creation, working on the front line of physical formation. Each elemental is charged with a specific mission regarding the assemblage, cohesion and animation of physical matter on Earth, ranging from the density of a mountain rock to the rarefied heat of a candle flame. They are created and programmed by a sublime hierarchy of advanced consciousness, who over aeons of time developed their Life Spirit to a point where they can create life itself — and give it away! This gift of life radiates down through the octaves of manifestation and condensation, and out into infinitesimal elemental parts. An expression from the elementals would sound like this: 'We know what we must do and we do it!'

Now let us take a look at the subquantum landscape of the new ether physics, as described by Dr Paul LaViolette, and consider the potential similarities between the elemental described above and the subquantum particle called the *etheron*: 'Subquantum kinetics proposes the existence of a primordial transmuting ether composed of subtle "etheron" particles. These continually react with one another in prescribed manners and also diffuse through space. Potentially, there may be many subquantum reactions taking place in the transmuting ether, but only a few of these may be important for describing the origin of the fields composing the matter and energy of our universe.'[33]

And to the second question, 'What is a nature spirit?' The term 'nature spirit', or deva, encompasses a wide range of supersensible beings inhabiting the astral-etheric field of the Earth. They assist the angelic hierarchies in the unfolding creation process on Earth, and they assume the guardianship of all physical form. As a general rule, 'nature spirit' is the term used to denote an overarching spirit, or guardian spirit, whose purpose it is to oversee a legion of elementals in a specific object or location. For example, one would have an overarching nature spirit of a marsh, a forest or a mountain. Another example would be a nature spirit of a tree. A single tree, in supersensible terms, is in fact a collective noun. Using the generic names, it is maintained at its roots by gnomes, in its sap by undines, in its leaves by aeriform light from sylphs and in its seed formation by salamanders. Nature spirits mediate the cosmic forces raining in from above and the telluric forces working up from below. They are also responsible for preserving the memory of a location from its inner-world and terrestrial-forming activity of the ancient past to the more recent human history residing within it.

Expanding to a more universal view, a nature spirit can also be considered as one vast expression of a primary element. An example of such an awesome and all-encompassing view can be heard in Dorothy Maclean's audio piece entitled *Kingdoms in co-creation*.[34] As a founder member of the Findhorn Association and an advanced intuitive, she spends much of her time in direct communion with the elemental kingdom, and she is widely held to be an authority on the subject of the devic realms. In the following message she receives an awe-inspiring view of the mineral world throughout the cosmos. She received this message while holding and contemplating a small and beautiful stone. This is what an overarching spirit of mineral form conveyed to her:

> Yes, I whom you have contacted am concerned with vastly more than your planet, for I contain — or am connected with — mineral life existing in various stages throughout creation. Nature is full of paradox, and that as you seek contact with, what you consider is a lower form of life, you in fact contact a more universal being. The mind of man codifies and formulates, which is within its right and purpose, but forgets that all is one, that God is in all, and that basic substance, seemingly most devoid of sensitive consciousness, is held in its state of existence by its opposite — a vast consciousness — too vast for you to do more than sense its fringes and know that it extends beyond your present imagination. You realize, too, that dense matter is influenced in its make up by stellar energies. Reverence all life and emulate my patience!

The pure clean codes of mathematics and the laws of modern physics are often regarded as an efficient and necessary antithesis to the many fundamentalist visions and versions of God-the-Creator. Yet when we begin to explore the supersensible realms through the eyes of a great seer like Dorothy Maclean we can observe how these realms too have a graceful, pure, logical structure to them, albeit a more fluid and emergent one.

One of the main sticking points between mainstream and spiritual science is the level of consideration given to the subtle moulding power of human emotion and psychoenergetics.[35] In mainstream science, the power of human emotion and intention are rarely awarded the status of 'relevant substance' or 'contributory factor' when observing the fluctuating expressions of physical phenomena. In spiritual science, however, an articulate use of emotion and intention and a constant witnessing of our thinking-feeling states during a process of experimentation are regarded as essential tools of discernment and communication on the path of seership. An excellent example of the effects of focused human intention can be observed in the many experiments carried out by members of 'The Intention Experiment'.[36] This project was initiated by the renowned author, researcher and speaker Lynne McTaggart, and it is supported by an innovative team of scientists and psychologists from the UK, USA and Russia. At a local level they have successfully measured the group thought effect on both the growth of plants and the essential properties of water. At a global level, they have mobilized thousands of people from around the world to participate in experiments of focused prayer, aimed at lowering violence in a targeted, war-torn area.

The global impact of the collective emotion and psychoenergetics of humanity can also be seen in the emergence of extreme and inclement weather patterns. Weather is in part a reflection of the collective astral-emotional state of humanity and the Earth. It is an expression of the soul of the Earth imprinting an image of itself in the physical phenomena of the elements, as the author and anthroposophist Dennis Klocek so clearly underlines in the following statement: 'Weather phenomena are really expressions of the inner soul life of the Earth. The soul body is the part of the organism in which it experiences *feelings* for the collective energies in which the organism is embedded.'[37] He also emphasizes the mirroring quality of weather when he suggests that 'the climate is the interface in which the results of our efforts to attain higher consciousness are displayed for all of the cosmos to see and evaluate'.[38]

Our personal interaction with the world is, above all, a thought-and-emotion responsive experience, and it is the subtle power of directed human emotion and received feeling-states we will be exploring on our journey of interpreting the language and expression of the nature spirits.

*   *   *

'A chain of infinitely small beings is not mixed at random, but admirably organized in a chain of life where each link allows another to exist.'[39]

The nature spirits and elementals exist in a dimension and resonate at a frequency outside the 'bandwidth' of normal human vision. Therefore, in order to enter this bandwidth, it is advisable to become familiar with the language and imagery used to describe the workings of the elemental world and its inhabitants. Each of us will have our own personal experiences on the road to seership, and we need to nurture and honour our individual inner landscape. However, it is also of great use to have our initial experiences authenticated and confirmed by the recollections of those who have gone before us. Along with the content of this book, there is a recommended reading list included on page 163.

As we approach the borders of this hidden world, it is essential to ease our habitual demand for an immediate logical explanation of our perceptions, and to temporarily put aside the mechanical reasoning that underlies most interpretations of reality today. It would also be wise to clear the mind of cartoon images, sentimental Victorian prints and garden-centre statues that have become associated with the form of the nature spirits in our modern age. However, it is worth noting that no matter how disingenuous these comic representations of nature spirits appear, their very presence in our media is testimony to the fact that a spiritual truth cannot be extinguished – it will always emerge somewhere, somehow. A thick curtain of laughter, derision and occasionally fear has been wrapped around these beings for many centuries. The truth of their existence has been cordoned off from us by the scoffing materialist mind, and as such they have been confined to the pages of fiction or the novelty section of certain retail outlets. Although they are petrified in form, these images and accounts of the elementals are a representation of a spiritual world that was once a clear and conscious reality for our ancient ancestors. It still resonates behind visible nature today, albeit undetected and unrecognized by most of us, and it is true to say that our popular fairy tales and films have made use of all that is in existence.

So, why do the creators of popular fiction represent the nature spirits in these comical or sentimental humanoid forms? And, more importantly, why do many students of seership experience moments with the nature spirits in these forms? What is the nature of the process taking place? The answer lies in our ability to minutely witness our fluctuating feelings and to interpret the imagery of our imagination correctly. It is our working imagination, conditioned by images of ancient and classical art, that clothes the energies and entities in nature with a specific form. We pick up thought forms already existing within the collective consciousness of humanity and apply them to our initial experiences. Or, alternatively, if we view the process from another direction, the nature spirits who wish to communicate with us can also make use of the existing imagery available in the collective human consciousness. These thought forms are an established substratum – a living field, or layer, of communal memory and imagination in the supersensible world. They are utilized by many intelligent beings, both physical and supersensible, and they provide an essential link in the chain between the form and the formless. The key to a mature analysis of our supersensible experience lies in our ability to discern between the innately powerful images and sensations arising from a path of committed stillness, reverence and patience and the images formed by an impatient and over-excitable imagination which usually leads to an erroneous analysis of the observed phenomena.

When we turn our gaze towards the world of the nature spirits, it is essential to put aside our usual, compact view of reality – a view that is based on sense observation interpreted by the intellect. When we suspend our demand for immediate cognition and instant labelling, and we allow a fluidity of the senses to develop, we begin to 'think' with our feelings and 'feel' with our thoughts. Developing a discerning analysis of our thinking-feeling states is an essential step on the path to seership. A careful and considered widening of the imagination is also essential in order to accommodate this new supersensible reality.

The astral-etheric world invariably defies any attempt to pin its innate emergent quality down into a fixed vocabulary. Therefore describing the activity of an elemental being is always an exercise in terminology. But for a student of spiritual science, there has to be a starting point and that usually means grasping an intellectual concept. At a later date, after a period of focused observation and contemplation, the intellectual concept begins to melt into something more mobile and conductive, something very intimate and yet universal.

When describing an earth spirit, one would speak of their substance as being a *sensory intelligence* within solid matter. The substance of a water spirit can be described as a mixture of *dreaming and emotion* existing in the fluid elements of the Earth. The substance of an air spirit is an expression of *wishing and willing* existing within the light-filled gaseous element, and a fire spirit can be described as a carrier of *living warmth,* which ignites and oversees the process of reproduction. These are, of course, vastly reduced generalizations, but they do present a starting point on the journey to supersensible seership. In the following sections we will be going into greater detail regarding the substance and activity of the elementals within the four elements.

In the following section on the four elements I have chosen to incorporate a selection of quotations from the lectures by Rudolf Steiner entitled Harmony of the Creative Word. *Meditating on these quotations has had a direct and tangible effect on my ability to understand the fluid* mechanics of the etheric world. By contempl ting the contents of these remarkable lectures, and fully grasping the concepts and imagery contained within them, I have been able to look through a new lens into nature and see a multi-dimensional view of the building blocks of our physical reality. I have not only come to accept this living, intelligent reality behind the world of form as an experiential truth, but I have also come to understand how the forces of human thought and emotion can make an impact on this highly mobile and conductive dimension in myriad ways.

Once I had thoroughly digested the descriptive imagery of the elementals in Rudolf Steiner's accounts of the ether, and I had understood the impulses guiding these beings in the formative world, my cognitive faculties began to slowly awaken and flower. These accounts of the astral-etheric world are not only inspiring and beautiful; they also satisfy the demands of the logical mind, which often needs to see a 'cause and effect' process unfolding. With practice, I began to experience fleeting moments of attunement with the Law of Oneness, the Divine Essence that pervades all things, and I began to sense the creative processes behind the visible forms in nature. Of necessity, these moments were sporadic and of short duration at the beginning, while my antennae began to awaken and adjust to the new layers of supersensory form.

There are, of course, many subtle nuances within the Earth's etheric field, but I have chosen to introduce the ether in four sections to correspond with the four elements. The elementals of solid earth represent what is called the 'life ether', the elementals of fluids represent the 'chemical ether', the elementals of air and light represent the 'light ether', and the elementals of fire represent the 'living warmth ether'.

If you keep an open mind and permit the following concepts to enter into your thinking, and keep them free from prejudice and impatient judgement, you will eventually begin to experience a new set of coordinates and a new way of apprehending the natural world and its emergent dynamics.

The Spirits of Earth and the Life Ether (Gnomes)

The nature spirits, elementals or supersensible entities living in the realm of solid matter are called earth spirits or root spirits, and in folklore they are called gnomes and kobolds. In the language of spiritual science, they are the Earth's intelligence within physical matter, and they bear that intelligence throughout the subterranean strata of the planet. They inhabit the solid structures of our world and they play a vital role in the materialization and dematerialization of earthly substances. They are also considered to be the spiritual midwives of plant reproduction within the soil, and act as mediators between soil and plant root. In their particular domain of the ether they work to bring the mineral element of earth into a state of flux, in order to conduct it to the roots of plants. Until relatively recently in human history much of humanity lived in caves, which were of course in the middle of the domain of the gnomes and kobolds. With their natural atavistic clairvoyance, our ancient ancestors must have known the moods and manners of these beings intimately.

The gnomes are at their optimum state of well-being when they reside in or near metals, ores and crystals. They have no dense physical form as we understand it and they resonate at an octave *below* the bandwidth of human visibility. The gnome's body is made entirely of ether and gravity, and their extremely clever consciousness projects into physical matter. They are essentially a sensory organ of intelligence and knowingness. They instantaneously perceive and fully comprehend the material world around them. One could say that they know things as soon as they see them, or that they receive a 'concept' at the same time as a 'percept'. The gnomes do not have to work things out within a time-line via a process of reason and deduction in the same way we have to, and they reside and resonate in their etheric dimension of earth with a clear understanding of the ideas existing in and on the physical plane of this planet. The idea of an etheric 'unit' processing a concept at the same time as a percept behind the constructs of space-time is reflected in the following quotation from physicist Amit Goswami: 'Einstein's theory of relativity precludes instantaneous communication via signals. And yet, quantum are able to influence one another instantly, once they interact and become correlated through quantum non-locality.'[40]

Rudolf Steiner takes us further into the relationship between the earth elementals and the solid earth when he says: 'For the gnomes, the entire Earth globe is like a permeable, hollow space. They can go into it everywhere; rocks and metals do not prevent them from walking and swimming around – although there are no words in our language really to describe their kind of locomotion. They have an inner feeling or experience of the various ingredients of the Earth. They feel differently when they wander along a metal vein from when they go along a layer of limestone. They feel all this inwardly. They go through everything. They don't really have the feeling that the Earth exists, but they feel there is a space in which they have gold feelings, or mercury feelings, or silica feelings, and various other feelings. This is putting it in human language, not in gnome language. Their language is much more descriptive; and they acquire this pronounced intellectuality ... through running along all the veins and strata for as long as they live. They acquire their comprehensive knowledge in this way, for the metals and the Earth reveal to them what is outside in the cosmos.'[41]

The relationship between planets and metals appears frequently in the western esoteric traditions; gold is regarded as a solar substance, copper is ruled by Venus, lead by Saturn and so on. All the rocks, stones and minerals on Earth are ultimately the offspring of the stars and they hold a memory of their stellar origins within them. In the ancient mystery centres, the physical planets were seen as the outer garments of exalted spiritual beings, and the corresponding metals on Earth were seen as physical expressions of their divine creative deed, enacted during the long process of condensation and separation of the planetary spheres within our solar system. The Earth's planetary spirit, Gaia, lives in fellowship with all the other planetary and stellar spirits, and the gnomes, while they are bound into earthly matter, gather and retain a direct knowingness of these mysteries.

The earth spirits are also a component part of the will of gravity; they are an adhesive between spirit and matter, gravity and levity, and they fashion the solid structures of our planet. They regulate the formative forces of the Earth in such a way that matter fills their living space of potential, or life ether, in countless expressions of highly finished physical, wrought work. They are a world sensory intellect inhabiting all physical form, and they have an inner sensory understanding for the many substances of the Earth. This experience we can only really compare, in human terms, with the inner cognitive nature of the human eye and the human ear. An example of this cognitive nature in action would be as follows. In the case of a plant, the gnomes would simultaneously apprehend and comprehend a specific field of activity resonating with ideas relating to the plant's formation, design and utility. In many indigenous communities around the world, the shamans and medicine men still work with the plant spirits, for the purpose of healing specific maladies within their community. Plant essence energy-medicine is now an increasingly popular complementary therapy, because it addresses the core emotional imbalance behind many physical ailments.

In the following quotation, Rudolf Steiner describes how the gnomes 'are entirely *sense* and it is a sense which is at the same time *intellect*, which does not only see and hear but immediately understands what is seen and heard; it not only receives impressions, but everywhere also receives ideas... Thus the gnomes are actually the bearers of the ideas of the universe inside the earth... We should look into the depths of the Earth, not to find abstract ideas or the mechanical laws of nature, but to see the wandering, meandering gnomes who are the light-filled preservers of world intelligence within the Earth.'[42]

This observation then begs the following question: If the gnomes exist in solid forms like rock, ore and plant roots, how are they able to receive the ideas of the cosmos? What does this actually mean? Again we can turn to Rudolf Steiner's view of the earth elementals for an answer. 'As sense organs they not only receive impressions from all sides but also ideas. We can indicate the way these root spirits receive their ideas. Plants shoot up out of the earth ... [They] come in contact with the extraterrestrial cosmos, and especially during certain seasons spiritual currents stream from the blossoms and fruits of plants down into the earth to their roots. And just as we turn our eyes towards the light and see, so root spirits turn their organs of perception to what trickles down to them from above through the plant and into the earth. And what trickles down to them is what the light has sent down into the blossoms and what the sun's warmth has sent into the plant, also what the air has done in the leaves and what distant stars have done in shaping the plants. Plants collect the secrets of the universe and sink them into the earth, and the gnomes take in these secrets of the universe from what trickles spiritually through the plants. And as they wander through the ores and rocks in the autumn through the winter, and carry what has trickled down to them through the plants, they become thereby those beings of the Earth who in their wandering carry the ideas of the whole universe through the Earth.'[43]

A plant is like a receiver dish; it absorbs information and light from the Sun and the planets of our solar system, and also the stars beyond. This great dance of the cosmos radiates into the plant world during the summer months when it is absorbed into the fully unfurled foliage. Then later in the year, during autumn, the cosmic narrative recorded in the foliage begins to filter down into the Earth where it is preserved in the matrices of crystals and ores. Gathering this universal information into themselves, the earth spirits then resonate and stream through their domain of the inner Earth, bearing with them all that has come down from the starry heights. They bear one world of form over into another, be it from one season to another, or from one epoch to another. They are above all the preservers of continuity in solid structures through the course of evolution.

It is important to remember that in order to maintain this continuity, the earth spirits have to *embody* gravity. In this next quotation from Rudolf Steiner, we learn how: 'The gnomes bind together ... all existing gravity, and they form their bodies out of this fleeting, invisible gravity, although the bodies are in continual danger of falling apart and losing their substance. The gnomes have continually to create themselves anew from gravity because they are always in danger of losing their substance. So, they must continually pay attention to what is going on around them, in order to save their lives. A gnome is more attentive to what goes on in the Earth than any other being.'[44]

In essence the gnomes are the life ether of the planet. They are an attentive, intelligent sense organ expressing the gravity, levity and integrity of physical form on Earth, including the gravitational pressure working into the surface, the geomantic currents operating beneath the surface, and the guardianship of plant germination and root formation within the living soil. In order to do, and be, all these things, they have to maintain an unceasing movement and expression of *becoming*, and the nature of this movement is born out of a kind of resistance towards the Earth. It is this continual gesture of thrusting away from the Earth that determines the upward direction of plant growth. The downward thrust of gravity pushes the plant root into the earth and the upward gesture of levity draws the plant up through the four states of matter, from the predominantly mineral element in the roots, to the watery element in the sap and leaves, into the aeriform-light and colour of the flower, and finally emerging into a generative heat in the fruits and seeds.

If we turn our attention to the field of theoretical physics and look for a unit that might correspond to the earth elemental or gnome in spiritual science, we come to the concept of the *graviton*. Considered to be an elementary particle without mass or charge, a graviton is presented by the new ether physics as a mediator, or carrier, of the force of gravity in the quantum field. From a certain standpoint, a gnome and a graviton appear to be one and the same thing; they are both a constituent part of gravity and they both appear to provide a coherent adhesive between spirit, ether and matter. However, the observations of spiritual science take us further. By looking beyond the imperative of the graviton to mediate the force of gravity, we learn how the earth elemental or gnome represents a constituent part of a vast supersensible intelligence with a traceable esoteric history.

Spiritual science points to a world where every atomic and subatomic particle, and every wave of energy in the whole of Creation, can be regarded as intelligent life. It has the potential to fill the many gaps existing between the fragmented and often contradictory theories that constitute the unified field theory today. However, this potential will only be realized if the mainstream scientific researchers of today are able to acknowledge the existence of a spiritual world, without equating it with religious extremism, New Age woo-woo or speculative pseudo-science. In the following statement, Dr William Tiller reveals three major stumbling blocks which continue to inhibit many mainstream scientists from taking a leap of exploration into the possibility of an intelligent, conscious ether, and from seriously contemplating the existence of a multi-dimensional spiritual reality beyond. He says: 'The greater limitation is the entrapment of the orthodox physics community by (1) their great expertise in specific areas of orthodox specialization, (2) their great *hubris* in thinking that they have all the relevant answers and (3) their great fear for their hard-won reputations if they are seen by their scientific peers to give serious credence to "outside-the-box" experimental data or theoretical thinking.'[45]

The word 'spirit' has been misused and distorted in many ways over the centuries and it is in great need of a re-framing and a rebirth. Anthroposophy has been at the forefront of this rebirth for over a century, and it has sought to focus this vital word into our social, philosophic and scientific vocabulary without the divisive and distorted charge of the past.

When we consider the supersensible activity of the earth spirits, it is important to remember that the elementals, and especially the gnomes, have no moral responsibility, ego or free will with regard to their earthly deeds. This is because they are continually being charged and programmed to participate in the creation and moulding of matter by the hierarchies who gave birth to them. In the following quotation by renowned biodynamic expert Manfred Klett, we see how the elementals depend not only on the morality of the hierarchies who create and influence them, but also on the directed will of human beings. 'When we expose our will in work we affect their realm. So the elemental beings depend on what kind of morality they meet, and can be servants of both good and evil. We are only able to fulfil our responsibility to the Earth and the environment if we know about these elemental beings, and deliver moral impulses to them. Imagine therefore how vital it is to really build up a personal relationship to nature.'[46]

Manfred Klett's observations underline how the elementals, and especially those responsible for the shaping of solid matter, can be compelled into service by the many conflicting forces influencing our world today. With the rise of the corporate, military-industrial complex over the last century, we have seen how the elementals of earth have been ruthlessly diverted and compressed into large-scale human mis-creations. They have been enslaved by a powerful and corrosive force which bears the outward logo of many a transnational corporation. The destructive deeds enacted by many of these corporations in 'service-to-self' have been born out of a remorseless, materialistic belief that the Earth is an inanimate object to be plundered and abused at will — a belief that is at complete odds with the divine hierarchical will, which is to be 'of service to all life-forms on Earth'.

However, like all beings, the nature spirits and elementals are endeavouring to evolve into higher states of being, and their continual enchantment and release into and from matter is their designated route back to higher Devachan (see pages 29 & 32). Viewed from the lofty heights of the higher hierarchies, humanity's continual incarnation into, and release from, matter, is also seen as *our* designated route back to the spiritual dimensions from whence we came. The perceived evil perpetuated by a ruthless, corporate elite with world-domination as its agenda seems to have been allowed to exist in order that it could perpetually invade our free will and thus ignite movement and growth within us. This fearsome mandate driving our evolution is encapsulated in the following statement by Rudolf Steiner: 'Men speak of good and evil, but they do not know that it is necessary in the great plan that evil, too, should come to its peak, in order that those who have to overcome it should, in the very overcoming of evil, so use their force that a still greater good results from it.'[47]

It is clear that the gnomes are compelled to participate in the wrought work of humanity's collective imagination. However, the difference between our sensory response to a Bernini statue bathed in sunlight and what we might feel in the presence of a concrete nuclear power plant is unmistakable. But what is actually triggering this sensory response beyond a subjective affirmation of taste? It is essentially the resonance and dissonance emanating from the elemental beings maintaining the integrity and structure of the solid form. The marble statue expresses man's highest artistic endeavour to imprint an image of himself in solid form, and it enables the elementals to participate in an act of artistic grace. The nuclear power plant, however necessary it may seem to be in the midst of a global energy crisis, expresses a blighting attack of hard angles formed from a disharmonious combination of substances in which the elementals are emanating a tangible, perceivable dissonance.

Some of today's advanced technologies could be viewed as a form of high magic, and yet many of the 'magicians' who preside over the 'altar' of such sophisticated, technical advances have little or no interest in following a path of sacred inner development; humanity, the Earth and all her life forces are regarded as mere resource. The time has come to remember a process of respectful ritual, where we harmonize our consciousness with the materials and phenomena we are about to work with. In the following quotation by René Querido, author of *The Golden Age of Chartres*, he emphasizes how, during the building of the cathedral, 'Even to take part in the construction one had to have a certain dedication to an inner life ... labourers were assigned tasks commensurate with their inner development as well as skill in the craft ... master builders understood that all construction was a transformation of earth forces, a sacred task.'[48]

In the future, beauty will increasingly become a moral force. Combining beauty with utility has to become one of the real accomplishments of our generation and the generations to come. Architects and builders who choose to cultivate an understanding of the elementals can and will receive profound inspiration from them regarding the improvement and alignment of civic, communal spaces. In the future, new construction methods will develop in line with the emerging transformational process taking place in the various densities of earth. The timing of these developments is dependent on our rise in consciousness and the moral responsibility that goes with it.

If we choose to develop a heightened sensitivity to the living intelligence within nature, we will in time improve all expressions of human endeavour, from architecture and transport to food and wine production. A sensitive collaboration and a co-creative relationship with the elemental kingdom is our way out of the dangerous environmental impasse we have arrived at today. The celebrated biodynamic wine grower Nicolas Joly emphasizes the importance of sensitive placement when he compares the old wine cellars of the past to the modern, sterile spaces of today. He reminds us how, '... reinforced concrete replaces the profound resonances of stones cut by masons who had the knowledge of polarities, and placed the stones accordingly in the direction they had before being quarried... Sealed into walls, they found again the magnetic pathway of the vibration of this north-south magnetic current in which they had been bathed since the beginning of time.'[49] He then goes on to describe how the care and attention given to telluric and geomantic properties within a cellar have a direct, calculable effect on the fermentation of wine. If the same care and attention is given to the geomantic and etheric forces beneath, and within, our future homes and civic buildings, the atmospheric resonance of our public meeting places will improve immeasurably.

At this crucial turning point in our history, humanity is preparing to take an evolutionary leap. The dormant strands of our DNA are being stimulated by a new wave of consciousness entering the Earth, and we are being given a unique opportunity, both individually and collectively, to develop into a more advanced species. If we choose the path of enlightenment, we will in time attain supersensible perception of the elementals of the earth. They are ready and willing to assist us in all things relating to solid structure. In our turn, we have to withdraw our customary insistence on a sense-based linear logic, and widen our imagination to accommodate their reality. If we show ourselves willing to acknowledge their existence, they will in the course of time allow us to enter their world-creating intelligence. The benefits deriving from such an interaction will be far reaching and joyous, but it is up to *us* to reach out to *them*. While the results of their activities may affect our lives in dramatic and traumatic ways, via extreme events like earthquakes and floods, they cannot force a dialogue with us – they do not have the free will to do so. We are the beings endowed with the grace and challenge of that volatile gift, and we are the ones who must now exercise it with a new earthly wisdom and devout responsibility.

*   *   *

It is an established tenet that all matter is made up of atoms, and at a quantum level an atom is comprised of 99.9+ per cent 'empty space'. Astrophysicists have established that it is only a minute percentage of the mass of the entire universe that consists of the kind of 'luminous' matter we can actually see. The solidity we experience in the material world is created by the electromagnetic fields emitted by the electrons in each atom, i.e. the negatively charged electrons within the atoms of our hand repel the similarly charged electrons of the atoms of the object we are touching. In theory, if the velocity of the electron fields were to be temporarily turned down, one would no longer be bound by gravity, things would become lighter and more malleable, and the opportunity to walk through solid stone would become a terrifying but exciting possibility. Indeed, it would be an opportunity to enter the domain of the gnomes in the hollow spaces of earthly matter.

An interaction with the earth spirits

In the following recollection, I have chosen to describe an interaction with the elementals of a large standing-stone overlooking my home in mid-Wales. I experience the nature spirit of this standing stone as an individuality whose purpose it is (a) to oversee the activity of a plurality of elemental beings, (b) to maintain the physical outline of the stone, and (c) to hold the stone's component parts of mass and energy at a specific octave of density. The vast amount of energy and supersensible 'will' needed to hold a heavy standing stone in its form and integrity on the face of the Earth can be felt and understood with great clarity in the presence of such a nature spirit. Without such awesome deeds of will, sacrifice and, above all, love, the physical world would disintegrate.

Through a regular, focused meditation based on the mantra 'I and the stone are one', united with an attitude of veneration and gratitude, I send out a heartfelt petition to the earth elementals to reveal the wisdom of their activity within the standing stone. I then wait in an attitude of receptive stillness and patience. Sometimes the stone is mute, stern and unresponsive, and sometimes it repulses human petition. When it is in a neutral or responsive phase I am able to enter a fleeting sensation of simultaneous apprehension and comprehension, and I can sense the fringes of the universal directive programming the elementals of the stone. I experience the space-time field slow down substantially and I experience myself becoming very much more porous. The directed intent of the mantra, and the power of love and veneration sent into the stone eventually brings forth a specific, sensory response; it is as though the electrons in both myself and the stone are becalmed – we both seem to become less solid. It is at this point that I begin to grasp some part of the nature of the interface between consciousness and matter. I am able to apprehend the space within and between matter, while at the same time comprehending some part of the ringing, thrumming intelligence reso-nating within this specific 'stone-space'.

In the tones of this thrumming Word, live the directives of the planets and stars above, and the will of Gaia from the inner Earth below – they combine to influence the vector of the torsion waves and the living space of potential in which the apparently solid-state matter of the standing stone resides. At certain times and in a certain light I am able to see a long, delicate spiral of light spinning above the stone.

During these moments of communion, I feel as though I am being allowed to read the Secret Book of Nature ... I am being granted a fleeting experience of the domain of the gnomes.

An example of a message, or 'gift of enhanced comprehension', from the elementals of the standing stone would translate as follows: 'We have been in existence here for millennia. Your veneration, gratitude and belief in the elemental kingdom has opened a way for you to experience *the supersensible reality you have come to understand through the mechanism of your intellect, and through the witnessing of your feeling life. Indeed it is really the higher aspect of YOU which has allowed 'you' to experience the living reality of US.'*

The Spirits of Water and the Chemical Ether (Undines)

From the world of crystals, ores and minerals we now turn our attention to the domain of the water spirits. The water spirits or undines, nymphs and nixes, as they are called in folklore, exist in the flowing, moist and watery elements on Earth. In spiritual science they are identified as the world chemists. They are responsible for the chemical ether within the totality of Earth's etheric body; without them, there would be no transformation of substances. The chemical ether can be regarded as the life force behind the coalescing and dissolving of the moist element on Earth.

The inner nature of the water spirits differs from that of the earth spirits – they are not so alert. They do not possess that ever-present, attentive intelligence of the gnomes, and they cannot address themselves to the whole airy cosmos with the same innate clarity as the gnomes. The undines are more akin to a highly receptive field of rapidly changing emotion, and their etheric substance is closely related to human feeling and dreaming. In the following passage Rudolf Steiner gives us an indication of this inner watery nature:

> We may be pleased by a red rose ... but these beings [undines] are able to accompany the rose saps which rise up to the rose blossom. There they experience the red of the rose blossom. They feel the processes of the world in a much more intimate way than we do. We remain outside of things with our feelings, but they live in the midst of events and participate in them... Whereas with our intellect we are like the elemental beings in solids, in our feelings we are more like the elemental beings that live in fluids. The undines stream through the tree in its sap; they and their feelings stream into every leaf. They not only perceive red and blue from the outside, they experience these colours inwardly; they experience sensation inside things. Thereby these spiritual beings have a much more intense feeling life, just as the gnomes in solids have a very intense intellectual life.[50]

When the bright shades of green emerge from the land in springtime, certain nature forces descend from the cosmos and draw out what has been active in the ground over the winter – it is as though the inside of the Earth unfurls itself and catches a glimpse of the heavens and the surrounding world. With sprouting and root development under way, the earth spirits *inform* the water spirits hovering above ground of the impending growth. The undines then focus their intense dream activity around the emerging plant, and in cooperation with the light-bearing activity of the air spirits they create a potent, living space for the leaf, stem and flower to materialize. They 'dream' the plant into physical form through the chemical ether. The undine's dream is a prequel to plant formation above ground and Rudolf Steiner describes this process in the following passage:

> The gnomes t'rust the plant entities upward. They would wither above ground if the undines didn't approach them from all sides and prove themselves to be world chemists with this dreamy consciousness in which they buzz around the plants. Undines dream the combining and separating of substances. And this dream into which the plants live, this undine dream into which the plants grow when they grow upwards from the ground, this is the world chemist that brings about the mysterious combining and separating of substances in the plant world, proceeding from the leaves. So, we can say that the undines are the chemists of plant life. They dream of chemistry.[51]

The undines have an extremely delicate spirituality, which is in its true element wherever water and air combine. They live entirely in the moist element, and they are especially active on the surface of drops or other bodies of water. Their presence is particularly strong where water, rocks and plants come together. To contemplate the whirling foam and rushing eddies of a waterfall after a rain storm is to truly feel the presence of the undines. To observe the mist rising from a river valley and see it metamorphose into a fine vapour is to experience the deeds of the undines. They yield themselves up to the movement and activity of the whole cosmos in their watery element, binding and releasing the substances in the air. They are continually changing and metamorphosing, and can best be symbolized as a fleeting chain of cloud formations. As they bind and release themselves into the fluid element, they urge the re-pre-cipitation of water into the Earth's atmosphere and they dream their life-mist around the plants of the earth.

When we choose to develop a heightened receptivity to our surroundings and allow a new mobility of soul within ourselves, the intense feeling life of the undines will begin to reveal itself. Sensing the feeling life of the watery element in our environment is an essential exercise on the path to supersensory seership. As we contemplate the undines rising with the plant saps and streaming into the leaves and flowers, and we take time to observe them expanding into cloud formations, a new heightened experience of living colour, momentum and growth will begin to reveal itself to us. When we think with our feelings, feel with our thoughts and acknowledge the existence of water spirits, they begin to reveal the hidden mysteries behind the transformation of substances. For those who practise the requisite attitude of soul-quiet and develop the heightened levels of receptivity needed to sense this domain, a profound nature-wisdom and world chemistry lies waiting to be discovered and, in time, maybe a meeting with the overarching Spirit of Water. But before reaching such a high-level meeting, we can move some way towards understanding the dream of the undines if we look with new eyes into the heart of an oak tree and imagine the sap rising, or gaze into the ripples of a clear water lake and say, 'Water Spirit, I allow your world wisdom to flow through me and I welcome it with grace.'

The undines and water spirits wish to assist and guide us in all matters to do with hydrology. The design and placement of new canals, dams and treatment plants would improve immeasurably if we were to embrace a true understanding of the supersensible nature of water. The following quotation comes from Phil Sedgman on the Living Water Flowforms' website: 'Water in its natural state does not travel in straight lines, it loves to meander and spread itself out. When water moves too fast, as it does in a "straightened" river, or when it is forced out of its natural meander patterns, as in hydroelectric dams or in water pipes, or when it is polluted, it loses its vortex patterns and its vitality.'[52] Our utilities could work in harmony with the entire eco-system, if they were built with an experiential knowledge of the esoteric forces working within the super-sensitive nature of water.

An accurate understanding of the chemical ether and its elementals is essential if we are to halt the deterioration of our precious water supply and restore it to its pristine quality. By implementing innovative designs like the lemniscate Flowform[53] in the field of hydrological engineering, we can take a decisive step towards healing our hard-working water. The life force of the elementals currently 'enduring service' within the many water-based industrial and municipal facilities on our planet could be considerably strengthened by (a) a recognition of their existence, (b) an understanding of their true nature, and (c) an honouring of their deeds.

The skilled seers of today are able to gauge the health and vitality of water through their communion with the undines. An example of such a seer is the author and anthroposophist Verena Stael von Holstein. She has provided many thought-provoking insights into the activity of the elementals in her book *Nature Spirits and What They Say*, and in the following passage she gives an example of a message conveyed to her by a nature spirit of water: 'For you, water is mostly something soft. When you consider water from the inside however, it has something totally structured about it. Water looks like a network of rods, nothing but rods. Coloured rods. Structures of sound which are spatial ... you have to imagine yourself as being inside the music, coloured, spatial music.'[54]

This view conveyed to Verena by the water spirit correlates with the findings of Japanese visionary and scientist Masaru Emoto. Dr Emoto has conducted a long and detailed study of the crystalline structures of water, and he has closely observed the effect our emotions and expressions have upon their appearance. He begins his experiments by setting an initial condition; this may include the use of sound, a focused emotional attitude or even a person's name. He then freezes the molecules of water which have been exposed to these varied conditions, and examines them under a dark field microscope with photographic capabilities. The highly responsive nature of water, with its ability to retain and record sensory information, is revealed in the many photographs of water crystals he has taken over the years. He has conducted experiments using a wide range of initial conditions. These conditions include projecting words and thoughts into the water and writing specific words like 'thank you', or 'You fool!' on the water container. In each case the design and structure of the frozen water crystals reveal a response from the supersensible world. Until recently, we have been unable to deliberately reveal this etheric tableau in the physical world of form. Dr Emoto's photography provides crystalline, physical evidence of the hidden power behind our thoughts and words, and their ability to mould our physical reality. The message from water is so simple: beautiful thoughts, words and deeds manifest beautiful, balanced and harmonious crystalline forms, and of course beautiful crystals within our body contribute to physical and emotional well-being.

Dr Emoto's most famous photographs show the influence of music on the inner structuring of water. As water freezes to the music of Mozart and Beethoven its crystalline structures develop into beautifully formed geometric patterns, while the water subjected to violent heavy metal music or aggressive rap distorts into blurred, lopsided formations. Water from mountain springs freezes into exquisite hexagonal forms, while city tap water is unable to form any coherent shapes. This is because it has been energetically compromised by the maltreatment it receives in the processing plants. A conscious communion with the undines and an increased use of Flowforms would be a decisive step towards retuning and returning tap water to a pristine, health-bearing state. (Further study of Dr Emoto's work is highly recommended.)[55]

Water rises from the earth and falls from the sky, it covers the surface of four-fifths of our planet, and we revere it as much for its soft, flowing, life-giving property as we fear its awesome and destructive power. It is the great messenger, forever circulating between the realm of pure forces in the sky and the rocky caverns below. At the interface between sea and air, water yields itself up to the heat and loses its attraction to the earth. As it rises with the warm air and expands into the atmosphere, it moves further away from earthly influence so that it may capture the soul narrative of the upper atmosphere. As the air cools, this narrative is then 'earthed' into ice crystals formed around minute dust particles and carbon dioxide molecules. The undines then feel the pull of the earthly attraction and begin their descent from the airy regions. They carry with them 'news' from the upper realms, which they send into the soil and rocks below. They are continually yielding themselves up to the rhythm of suction and sublimation that constitute the breath of the soul of the Earth.

Our ancient ancestors revered water as a gateway to the inner and upper planes, and the art of scrying or divination through the element of water was a staple practice for the shamans or priests of a tribe. They understood that water carried memory and, in essence, this form of divination was an intentional communion between the shaman and the elementals of water. The received images and sensory responses were then interpreted and acted on accordingly. As Dennis Klocek so clearly emphasizes in the following quotation: 'Nature spirits, or elemental beings were linked to humans and weather through the mutual interpenetration of the human body and weather systems with the forces and formative patterns of rotations of the elements. Magical practices for controlling the weather arose from those connections.'[56]

Our language is full of references to the receptive nature of water; phrases like 'welling up with emotion', 'feeling overwhelmed' and 'an undercurrent of emotion' are well established images in our daily communications. We even produce water from our eyes, as tears, in response to a wave of emotion surging through our body. Water is alive and responsive to our thoughts and emotions, because in its inner nature it *is* emotion. With this spiritual truth anchored into the material world so conclusively by Dr Emoto's work, we are faced with an urgent imperative to raise our consciousness above the flow of resentments and negativity that so often dominate our thinking life. The famous Siddha Yoga teacher Swami Muktananda was once asked why he believed people in the West suffered such poor health. His answer was simple and to the point: 'Bad Mantras!' So many of us are locked into the competitive structures of our society, and the daily content of many a western, materialistic mind consists of an endless aggregation of data infused with worry, anger and contention. Such negative internal mantras inhibit healthy cell regeneration and distort the crystalline forms in our bodily fluid.

The undines are responding, second by second, to every thought and feeling we choose, so the simple act of choosing a better feeling thought has life-changing consequences for ourselves and our environment.

* * *

Messages from the spirits of water

My first physical sighting of a water nature spirit occurred one summer evening while I was contemplating the ripples on the surface of a spring-fed lake in the uplands of mid-Wales. The beams of sunlight glinting on the waves defined a glittering path across the centre of the lake, and I fell to deeply musing the wonder and generosity of the element of water, without which our planet would be a bleak and lifeless desert. I began to send out a pulse of heart-felt gratitude along the glittering, sun-lit runway, while inwardly repeating the mantra 'My true self and the lake are one'. After a while a thin veil of cloud covered the sun and the glinting runway mellowed into a more muted glow. At this point, I started to discern a shimmering lilac haze gathering over the centre of the lake, and after a short while it began to organize itself into an approximately 20-foot high vertical form of intense colour, oscillating between supersensible and visible reality. Every cell in my body was tingling with a feeling of aliveness and anticipation; I knew that I beheld the overarching undine of the lake, and I knew that it was hovering at the border of visible reality in order that I might behold it in the rarefied substance of living colour.

I believe I was able to apprehend and comprehend this gracious visual gesture as a response to my heightened state of wonder and profound gratitude. My first unconscious urge was to rush towards the lake spirit with an outburst of joy! Yet at the exact same moment I also received a kindly but firm directive to stay back, find the centre point of my attention, sit in a state of equanimity and equilibrium, and quietly witness the shimmering grace of the moment. The message from this being was clear. That message has rung down the ages to aspiring seers the world over and is simply this: 'If you would gain power of sight – practise silence and stillness.'

The undine of the lake also gave me a valuable and generous insight into how a nature spirit can enter the bandwidth of human vision, by harnessing the living substrate of rarefied colour existing in the ether.

Another memorable interaction with the undines occurred when I received a powerful message from the water spirits of a large waterfall in north Wales. Wales has always enjoyed a climate of high rainfall, and the hills and valleys are full of streams and waterfalls. I particularly remember visiting one of the larger waterfalls in the north after a week of stormy weather. The sound of the water was deafening as it thundered over the precipice and crashed onto the rocks and boulders below. The sheer power and force of the moving water pulled me firmly into present-time, and it centred me in a heightened state of alertness as I sat on a rock amongst the eddies. I then set my intent for communication and began to repeat the mantra 'I and the water are one'. I sang long tones and songs of praise into the falling water. I allowed my eyes to relax into an all-inclusive vision, and when they no longer pinpointed a singularity they began to accommodate a plurality of activity with equal attention.

All around me there was a cacophony of noise, movement, activity and expression – life truly expressing itself in sound and action! I continued to penetrate this cacophony with my breath, my voice and my respectful petition for communication.

After a while a tunnel of supersensible vision began to open up. I moved into the unmistakable sensation of 'time out of time', and in this place of timelessness the eddies, flows and whirlpools began to slide into slow motion. The bubbles and foam and ribbons of water were clearly visible as separate entities, and they allowed me to observe and experience the 'mission of water as messenger' in its many shapes and forms. I not only felt the highly receptive field of changing emotion within the water forms with great clarity, I also felt a raw and painful pang of realization as the truly selfless, gracious, sacrificial nature of the water spirits was revealed to me. The undines carry the emotion of the world and its inhabitants from the earth to the sky and back again; they are forever cleansing, metamorphosing and communicating between the elements. As their sobering and tutelary transmission penetrated me a profound wave of gratitude swept though my physical body, and at that same moment I saw a salmon rise from the foam in front of me. Thrusting itself out of the element of water, writhing up through the element of air, its sleek, dark, silver-grey form was almost shocking against the white foam. Its message to me was . . . 'Human being, watch me rise! You came to Earth to learn to swim, to master the mighty currents of your emotions. Rise up from the eddies and whirlpools of conflict wrestling in your soul, and let your spirit soar.'

The Spirits of the Air and the Light Ether (Sylphs)

Moving on from the emotion-filled world of the water spirits, we now turn our attention to the next group of elemental beings who inhabit the element of air. In folklore, the air spirits are known as sylphs, elves, lemures or will-o'-the-wisps. The term, 'will-o'-the-wisp' gives an indication of the true nature of the air spirits because the inner nature of the sylph is related to human will – just as the inner nature of the undine is related to human emotion. Their consciousness lives in the airy element of the ether and they become enchanted into all forms of gas in the earthly realm. The sylphs are also the light-bearers in the etheric body of our planet. And just as the gnomes carry the *life ether* through the solid earth and the undines carry the *chemical ether* within the fluid element, so the sylphs convey the *light ether* through the element of air and bring it to bear upon the ripening processes in nature. The sylphs are sensitive to the alignments of the planets and they are highly receptive to the information radiating in from the sun. Their moulding activity in nature is influenced by the solar and planetary movements impressed into the Earth's atmosphere, and they are regarded as the beings who carry the universal will, love and wisdom of the cosmos into the airy element of Earth. Rudolf Steiner explains this mission in the following way:

> Their task is to lovingly convey light to the plant. And just as the undine is the chemist for the plant, so is the sylph the light-bearer. The sylph imbues the plant with light. Through the fact that the sylphs bear light into the plant, something quite remarkable is brought about. The light, that is to say the power of the sylphs in the plant, works on the chemical forces that were induced into the plant by the undines. Here occurs the inter-working of the sylphs' light and the undines' chemistry. This is a remarkable moulding and shaping activity. With the help of the upstreaming substances, which are worked on by the undines, the sylphs weave an ideal plant form out of the light. They actually weave the archetypal plant within the plant from light, and from the chemical working of the undines.[57]

At this point, it is important to fix the image of an 'archetypal or ideal plant form' in our imagination. Its function in the ether can be compared to that of a photographic negative or a living blueprint which informs the plant what it is and how it is to operate in its environment. It can also be seen as a supersensible frame that defines the plant's physical structure in space. In the autumn, this 'ideal form' sinks down into the earth with the retreating foliage and is taken up by the root spirits for the process of plant reproduction.

So, let us look at the essential being and nature of a sylph. Like the undines who rise with the saps and weave their chemistry in the moist element around the emerging leaves in springtime, the sylphs are also in a constant state of movement. Flashing like little meteors and shimmering like tiny shards of lightning, they flit over the earth, glittering and vanishing in an ever-spinning spiral between spirit and rarefied matter. The element of air is continually being impressed with an evolving solar and starry script, and the sylphs lovingly bear this shimmering, aeriform script into the plant kingdom, where the upturned gesture of welcome and longing eagerly absorbs the sylph-worked light. With trained occult vision, one can see the scintillating whorls of life pulsing in waves around the plant, each species receiving a specifically configured current of etheric life force in which its physical form is moulded. The sylphs embody something akin to a human wish which they 'will' into the earth via the aeriform expressions of life.

As the gnomes feel themselves most at home near crystals and ores, and the undines rejoice in the drenched moss and dancing spray of a waterfall, so the sylphs feel their deepest sympathy in the moving currents of air set in motion by a bird in flight. Most of us can remember a moment of utter delight at the sound of a small brown bird fluttering close by, or a flock of swallows flying overhead on a still, warm evening. And if we were to ask a bird who taught it to sing, the answer would be, 'Why the sylph, of course!' Our delight in these exquisite sounds is amplified by the ecstatic presence of the sylphs in the airy element. In the previous section on the water spirits, we saw how the interior structure of water appears to be a collection of colourful rods of music. This music also reverberates through the surging currents of air which ebb and flow through the atmosphere. It is a focused reverberation of the cosmic creative word in the airy element of earth, and the tones of this music are especially pure around the oscillations set in motion by a flock of birds. They create a wistful refrain within the world song, forever singing itself into form, and it is to this song that the sylph is irresistibly drawn.

Steiner describes this refrain of the sylphs in the following passage:

> When in the spring or fall you see a flight of swallows, which is setting the air in motion through its passage, this moving air stream around each bird is something that can be heard by the sylphs; they hear cosmic music sounding from it. Or if you're travelling by boat, and seagulls fly out to it, their flight produces a spiritual sound, a spiritual music, that accompanies the ship. Again it is the sylphs who live in these sounds, who have their home in these moving air streams. They live in the spiritually resounding, moving, airy element, and they experience what the power of light sends into these oscillations of the air...[58]

When a sylph senses a bird in the air, a very special feeling, or wish, comes over it. While a sylph does not have an ego like a human being, it experiences something akin to an ego feeling when it spirals into the whirlwinds and currents set into motion around a bird in flight. The sylphs also feel this sense of 'I am' when they track the flight of a bee. They tuck into the air-stream around the bee and accompany it to the waiting blossom. To observe the meeting between bee, blossom and pollen on a supersensible level is to behold a small, light-filled etheric aura hallowing a sacred, creative deed. The sylphs work closely with the fire spirits in the space around a flower blossom; it is an intimate working of light ether and warmth ether, as the sylphs bring light for maturation and the fire spirits bring living warmth for seed production. It is similar to the intense, intimate cooperation between gnomes and undines during early spring, when the young shoots are thrust into the moist surface air hugging the ground, or the interaction of the undines and sylphs in cloud formation. There is always an influx of elemental activity when animals and plants engage, whether the engagement is between a bee and a flower, a cow and her pasture or a boar and his roots – theirs is an ancient relationship, and an ancient understanding exists between the two kingdoms.

As the summer unfolds, the sylphs press down into the plant world with an ever-increasing intensity, bearing their living light into the leaves and flowers. They are intimately connected with the maturing process in nature, and all ripening and maturation in the natural world would fail to come about if these beings did not exist. They are compelled by the Sun and the rotation of the Earth to bear light into the plant and animal worlds. Then, later in the year, when the leaves begin to turn and wither, the light stored in the plants during summer begins to reflect back into the cosmos in shades of red, yellow and gold. As the foliage dies back, the sylphs are released from their enchantment into form, and they begin to surge back into the atmosphere, leaving behind their carefully woven ideal plant form, or etheric blueprint, to trickle down into the earth for future use in reproduction. The sylph bears the love of the cosmos into the building blocks of nature, so that it may perpetuate and resonate within the wrought work of the Earth.

The release of the sylphs from their enchantment into matter during the fall is a poignant, supersensible image. But this image is not just confined to the pages of esoteric literature; it also appears at the heart of the biophoton theory pioneered by Dr Fritz-Albert Popp.[59] The term 'biophoton' refers to the coherent photons emitted from all biological organisms, and Dr Popp has shown that this dynamic web of biophoton light is constantly being released and absorbed by the DNA in the cells of all living organisms. The structuring and regulating activity of this sensitive biophoton field seems to serve as the organism's main medium of communication with the surrounding environment, and also as the principal regulating force within the boundaries of its own body. When plants begin to wither and retreat into the soil, they release waves of biophotons. The ancients were well aware of this rhythm of coherent light in nature, and they recognized it as the activity of the sylphs.

There is another crucial dynamic to consider when we contemplate the absorption and release of biophotons or the enchantment and emancipation of the sylphs into and out of living organisms — the effect this activity has on the flow and fabric of time. So let us look into this more deeply. In Chapter 2 we learnt how Professor Nikolai Kozyrev, the pioneer of torsion field physics, worked with time flow detectors to determine the real-time position of stars. He also maintained that the pull of gravity could be impacted by the dynamics of a torsion wave. His use of sensitive time flow detectors revealed that a temporary slowing down and speeding up of time occurs when matter solidifies and disperses, for example when water freezes and melts. He also recorded a measurable speeding up of time when a plant begins to wither and release its biophotons, and a slowing down of time when it begins to grow and mobilize biophotons into coherence as the new cells are forming.[60]

Time and gravity are intimately entwined. In many ways they seem to be one and the same thing, and this revelation is clearly reflected in the wisdom of spiritual science. When we look carefully into the structure and designated responsibilities of the spiritual hierarchies, we see how the Archai, or Spirits of the Rotation of Time, have direct rulership over the gnomes and the earth elementals. This is because the gnomes are detachments, or offspring, of the Spirits of the Rotation of Time. The consciousness of an earth elemental is above all a component part of Earth's gravity, and just as the gnomes carry out the overarching will of the Archai, so the biophotons carry out the overarching instructions embedded in the torsion waves flowing into the Earth.

The very title 'Spirits of the Rotation of Time' implies a rulership over the angular momentum of time and torsion, and it leads to the idea of a unit of time being an intelligent entity in and of itself. This view is reflected in the experiments carried out by Professor A.I. Veinik of the Belarus Academy of Science. According to his theory, every substance has it's own 'chronal charge' defined by the quantity of 'chronal' particles surrounding it. He calls these particles 'chronons'. Through his experimentation with gyroscopes, Professor Veinik has found that strong 'chronal' fields can be generated by spinning masses. While an object is spinning, its chronons are interacting with chronons from the surrounding chronal field and the weight of the object changes. According to A.I. Veinik's theory there are two types of chronons, a 'plus' and a 'minus' chronon, and the sign of the chronon depends on the orientation of its spin.[61]

The chronon is yet another sibling to the graviton and the gnome, and together they spin down the great spiral of creation wielded by the Spirits of the Rotation of Time.

Like the graviton and the gnome, the biophoton and the sylph can be considered very close siblings in the dance of creation. The formation and maintenance of an 'ideal plant form' in the life cycle of a plant is a very significant movement in this dance, and if we follow the detailed observations of Rudolf Steiner we can learn how certain legions of the sylph kingdom are assigned to the creation of the ideal plant form, or coherent biophoton blueprint, during the months of spring and early summer. Then, later in the year, when the plant has flowered and fructified, the sylph-worked ideal plant form begins to sink into the earth for the duration of winter, taking the plant's memory and absorbed stellar narrative into the dark shelter of the soil.

As the gnomes follow the downward flow of gravity with root growth and the upward flow of levity with stem growth, so the sylphs must also follow the will of gravity and levity. From the light-filled currents of the upper atmosphere to the light-woven ideal plant form at ground level on the Earth, the sylph is constantly obeying the cosmic will of growth and metamorphosis.

In the past one hundred years the air spirits have had to work hard to compensate for the increasing pollution in the Earth's atmosphere. From excessive CO_2 and radio-waves to the more sinister manipulation of the atmosphere with barium salts, aluminium dioxide and other toxic compounds, known as chemtrail geoengineering, the many and varied pollutants are putting an enormous strain on the sylphs. Not only is there a decrease of oxygen in the air, there is also a decrease in the amount of pure sunlight reaching the Earth's surface, and the determining field of planetary alignments, which is continually raying in its directive from space, is being scrambled and distorted by atmospheric pollution. This inevitably hinders the etheric field around our planet and the well-being of all life on Earth.

In her communication with a nature spirit of air, Verena Stael von Holstein received the following information regarding air pollution:

> ... in the zone close to the plants we have an enormous increase in workload. And one of our most important tasks is to ensure the plants suffer as little as possible from air pollution. That means that in a very thin zone, thin as a sylph, the air around the plants is still good. That is why it's so much more pleasant to breathe in the wood. We do what we have to, and give the filth on to the water. And you [humans] don't just pollute the air, but also the light. Air pollution [is] at the same time a pollution of light. Wisdom corresponds spiritually to light and when the air is polluted through human deeds ... the wisdom of heaven in light reaches the Earth in a polluted form.[62]

At a later stage in this communication the subject of nuclear power stations was introduced, and the air spirit indicated that '... they ionize the air in such a way that inwardly the air has to vibrate – this makes the air nervous and nervous air isn't good'.

There are many things we can do to mitigate the damage inflicted on our eco-systems. In Chapter 8, methods and indications are given to help counteract the pollution existing in all four of the elements in our immediate environment. At this point, however, it is worth highlighting a suggestion offered by the messenger of air mentioned above. The messenger indicated that a focused, intentional prayer directed into the air can be a powerful alleviative, especially when it is spoken into rising whorls of incense. Incense is a gracious gift of resin from the trees, which in its airy form provides a medium for our prayers to become *visible* as well as audible in the supersensible world — the words are received by the angelic beings of air, then changed directly into their equivalent substance on a higher plane.

Although the angelic hierarchies wish to guide and assist us at this time, they cannot make incursions into the individual, free will of human beings — it is up to *us* to reach out to them. Only then can the spiritual hierarchies respond from the realms in which they dwell, and bestow on us the inspiration needed to initiate healing and change in the world of physical form. This vision of a visible prayer is a timely reminder never to underestimate the healing power of our consciously willed intention. As the sylphs embody a substance akin to human will, let us consciously include them in *our* directed will towards a positive transformation and healing of our beleaguered environment.

The work of the sylphs is expressed in countless deeds of virtuosity, from their enchantment into the scintillating whorls of life around a growing plant to the service they render the powerful nature spirits of the upper atmosphere. Vast troughs, ridges and air streams are set in motion by the harmonic resonances reaching into the Earth's atmosphere. The angular dynamics experienced with the other planets and the forces of the fixed stars drive the invisible turbines behind each great storm, hurricane and trade wind. The sylphs adhere to the directives set in motion by the fire spirits of the Sun; they blend with the heat and the levity-producing, expansive, evaporative tendencies wrought by solar flares and the seasonal movement of the Sun. They are continually phrasing their ceaseless 'movement of becoming' on the front line of weather creation, by expanding and contracting within the meteorological expressions set in motion by periods of solar and celestial perturbation and quietude. The sylphs are in service to the will of Gaia — a will that keeps disintegration and disorder at bay by continually absorbing and initiating checks and balances within the force fields of the Earth.

The sylphs carry the narrative of the cosmos from the rarefied forms of the upper atmosphere to the airy spaces within matter.

As the seasons advance from spring towards summer, the Earth increasingly gives up its soul content — elemental beings — to the cosmos. As they pass from the inner Earth out into the atmosphere, they fall under the sway of the stars again. It is part of our planet's mighty breathing process through the course of the year. Like our own human organism, there is a regular rhythm of inhalation and exhalation throughout the Earth's organism, and the peak of mid-summer is a time of optimum activity for the air spirits, as they are intimately linked into the great exhalation from the Earth. Rudolf Steiner explains this process in the following way:

> Everything in these beings that during the winter had produced a close relationship with the Earth itself now becomes related to the cosmos ... the elemental beings seek to escape from the Earth; and spring really consists of the Earth's sacrificial devotion to the universe in letting its elemental beings flow out into it ...

He then describes how we can, with heightened sensitivity, experience this exhalation of the soul of Earth, by saying:

> In the plant cover we have the physiognomy of the plant spirit. It is like gazing into the soul of the Earth — just as we gaze into the eyes of another person — if we understand how it manifests its soul in the blossoms and leaves of the plant world.[63]

This is why the festival of summer solstice was celebrated with such joyful singing and dancing by our ancient ancestors. They wanted to 'gaze into the eyes of Gaia' and inhale the exhaled soul of the Earth.

The glittering nature spirits of air bear the light and soul of the Earth through the atmosphere so that we may prepare ourselves to experience this great exhalation – they inspire devotion within us for the cosmic principle that lives in all earthly things.

Messages from the spirits of air

I have the greatest good fortune to share my upland home with a pair of red kites. I never tire of watching these beautiful birds of prey with their distinctive red tail feathers circle and soar above the house, and I never cease to wonder at their effortless grace as they gently descend onto the upper branches of the sycamore trees at the foot of my garden. They have such an intimate and responsive relationship with the moods and manners of the air – they are at all times united in ecstasy with it.

Yet, beyond the physical beauty and outline of the bird, what is it that excites such an ecstatic rush of gratitude and wonder?

It is the scintillating joy of the sylphs, as they yield themselves into the moving streams of air around each bird. It is the sylph worked spirals of airy light, multiplying and intensifying in the oscillations set in motion by the flight of the kites – these are the phenomena that transport me to the threshold of a supersensible experience.

So, the next time you are moved by the power and grace of a bird of prey in a clear blue sky, or you are enchanted by a flock of swallows soaring overhead, let your eyes rest on the moving airy element around the birds and listen carefully. Can you hear the cosmic tones just beyond the sound of beating wings? It is the song of the sylphs carrying the waves of tone and torsion across the airy regions of the Earth.

* * *

The elementals of air are under immense pressure to process the fallout from humanity's unconscious and wilful mistreatment of the environment, and one of the most poignant expressions of this stress can be experienced when harsh fertilizers are sprayed onto wild pasture land. The supersensible structure of the fertilizer chains the elementals to a uniformity, and it coerces them into a season of unrelenting, unitary growth. There is, above all, an overwhelming wave of utter weariness pervading the pasture after the spraying has been done, and the sylphs appear cowed and curled inwards. Instead of the vibrant whorls of sylph-worked light, the air is subdued and punctured with what I can only describe as fleeting dots of 'no-light', and an indefinable sorrow resonates in the background tones for a while before disappearing into the wind.

In complete contrast to the scene above, the uneven pasture land close to my home is only fertilized with natural manure, and during high summer it abounds with a myriad variety of wild grasses and flowers. When the Sun reaches the height of summer solstice, I see the flourishing, thriving grassland exude an aura of intense activity. In the midsummer Sun, I am able to discern the sylph-worked light radiating an aurora of oscillating shafts and spirals over the full-grown grasses and flowers, and there is a polyphony of rarefied supersensible sound resonating from the threshold of clairaudient tone.

This is the kingdom of nature expressing itself in harmony and health. This is the exhaled soul of the Earth expressing herself in contented tones of light and sound. I give thanks for the wonder, mystery and magic in all earthly life.

The Spirits of Fire and the Warmth Ether (Salamanders)

'Once fertilized, a flower drops its petals, releasing attachment to external appearances in order to become seed-bearing fruit. In our journey towards birthing a new reality, we, too, shed what no longer serves in order to shift from one stage of being to the next.'[64]

Stacey Robyn

Let us now consider the fourth group of elemental beings inhabiting that most rarefied of elements, the element of fire. They are most widely known as fire spirits, but in folklore traditions they are called salamanders. They are the oldest of the elementals and therefore their consciousness is the most developed. They are, above all, beings of transformation, and they know the sacred pathway from death and decay to rebirth intimately.

Before we consider their deeds within the rhythms of nature, let us examine the primal element of fire itself. Both the ancient alchemists and modern spiritual scientists consider fire to be a gateway to the spiritual world. A flame is something spiritual — nothing material can endure it. It is a doorway into the supersensible realms and we stand in front of it with reverence; this is why acts of ritual devotion commence with the kindling of a flame. Fire possesses an all-pervading quality and is so rarefied that it permeates each of the other elements. We can sense it in a warm summer wind, we can feel it in the hot springs gushing from the ground, and we can see it consume the solid forms of wood in the winter hearth. We behold its beauty from the outside and can feel its warmth within. It is not solely dependent on external touch. With a concerted meditative effort we can become vaguely aware of what is airy, watery and solid within our own organism, but with the element of fire we are constantly aware of how warm or cold we feel.

Fire is the great consumer and creator; it is forever recycling matter in the spiralling waveform between sensible and supersensible worlds. It can devour a forest in one voracious gasp, and yet concentrate its vast, creative power into a minute seed, igniting germination and new life.

Whether it is the awesome display of an erupting volcano or the hypnotic sway of a votive candle flame, fire has a compelling fascination for us. Its beauty, its movement, its unpredictability and the sound it makes never fail to arrest our attention. The crackling and hissing of an open fire seems to invite us to pause our chattering minds and enter into a dialogue with the being of fire itself. For many of us, an early childhood initiation is our first encounter with a flame.

In the following passage Rudolf Steiner introduces us to the threefold nature of fire — its light, its heat and its smoke:

> One might say fire is situated at the boundary between the per-ceptible, material world and the etheric, spiritual realm that is no longer perceptible. What happens to an object consumed by fire? Light is produced. In fact, heat, if it is sufficiently intense, pro-duces a source of light that is outwardly imperceptible, but which reaches upwards into the spiritual worlds. A part is given over to the invisible, but it must pay for this in the form of smoke. Out of the part that was first transparent and translucent, an opaque 'smoky' portion is separated off. So we see how fire or warmth is divided into two components. It divides itself off towards the light, thus opening up a path towards the supersensible, but as a result it also has to send something down into the opaque, per-ceptible, material world. Every form of existence has two aspects. Thus, where we have light as a result of heat we also find opaque, dark matter appearing. That is an ancient, basic teaching of spiritual science.[65]

This act of separation and densification is at the hub of all physical existence. In the Earth's far, far distant past, everything was fire; fire was the primal substance and every breath of air, every sparkling ocean and every rocky mountain is an expression of densified fire. Gold, silver and copper are densified fire, everything was born of fire! And to the question 'How do the exalted hierarchies produce solid matter as it exists on our planet?' Rudolf Steiner gives us the following answer:

> They send down elemental beings that dwell in fire, and imprison them in the air, water and earth. They are emissaries, elemental messengers of the spiritual, creative, formative beings. At first, elemental beings live in fire, and to put it pictorially, they feel comfortable there. Then they are condemned to an existence of bewitchment. We can say as we look around us, 'The beings

whom we have to thank for everything that surrounds us, had to descend from the fire element and are bewitched in the things of this world.'[66]

In the blossoming activity of nature, the fire spirits are weavers of living warmth. Their consciousness lives in the fiery element and their spiritual substance is the living warmth ether responsible for fructification. They collect the warmth generated on hot summer days and carry it into the plant blossoms in a similar way to the sylphs' collection of light. The domain of the salamanders is where the almost imperceptible pollen and the heady scent of a flower signifies the boundaries of dematerialization and a merging with the supersensible. Out of our five senses, it is our sense of smell that initially registers the most rarefied substance of a physical plant.

In the same way that the sylphs feel a deep sense of 'I am' when they sense a flock of birds in flight, the salamanders feel an even deeper sense of sympathy when they attach themselves to insects — especially the bees and butterflies. To watch a butterfly, immobilized by the cool morning air, slowly unfold its graceful wings to the rising Sun is to witness the work of the salamanders in the insect world. The light, airy quality of the sylphs is intensified into a more rarefied sphere, moving from light ether into a radiant living warmth ether. The luminous aura we see surrounding a bee and a butterfly is none other than a fire spirit accompanying it on its path from blossom to flower. The fire spirits feel the utmost sympathy for insects and wish to be completely united with them. As they hover over an insect wing, the salamanders are able to glide into the soft sheen of a summer blossom and weave their living, cosmic warmth around the carpel. They are the guardians and gatherers of generative warmth on the planet, and without them there would be no continuity of species.

Fire spirits are above all the preservers of seeds and germination in the kingdoms of nature. They weave their living, creative warmth for the purpose of reproduction, and they carry the seeds of the world from one generation to the next. If we look with spirit eyes into the reproductive cycle of the plant, animal and human kingdoms, we see that from the seed formation in a tiny violet to a nesting bird on her eggs, and to the heat generated for ovulation in a female human being, there is a perpetual repetition of the first fiery deed of creation echoing through time and matter. In the animal kingdom, the aptly termed phrase 'on heat' is given to the time of greatest potential for reproduction. The fire spirits are the guardians of this deed; they are the gatherers of warmth in the environment and within all organisms. They transform this warmth into the living heat needed for all ripening processes.

As the temperature rises in high summer and we anticipate the coming harvest, it is essential to see the earth as the plant mother and to see the sky as the father element. This truth was celebrated by our ancient ancestors, and was a basic core understanding behind their seasonal ceremonies. Today, however, it is important to grasp this knowledge with our modern intellect, as well as respecting it as traditional folk-wisdom. It is relevant for the nascent seer to understand the exact spiritual science working behind germination and reproduction. In an earlier section, we learned how the 'ideal plant form', or etheric blueprint, is woven out of chemical ether and light ether by the undines and sylphs. When conditions are right, this ideal form folds down into the earth, and awaits the coming of a seed imbued with warmth ether. The seed in the carpel is actually the male element of the plant and receives all that the cosmos, or 'Father Sky', has sent down to it over the summer. Rudolf Steiner explains this in the following way:

> The only fructification that occurs is between the cosmic seed in the blossom, containing the warmth which the fire spirits took from the cosmos, and the female element, namely the ideal form of the plant, which had previously trickled down into the Earth's soil and is resting there... Nothing that occurs above ground is connected with the plant's womb. The

motherly element, the ideal form of the plant, is carried down from the plant cambium between the bark or skin and the wood or pith. Fructification takes place under the earth during winter, when the seed enters the earth and meets the [ideal] forms which the gnomes have received from the work of the sylphs and undines.[67]

The work of the salamanders helps to 'minimize' the cosmos into a seed, enabling each plant to embed a picture of the macrocosmos in its microcosmic seed. The pollen provides a vehicle for the fire spirits to focus and carry the living, transforming warmth ether to the carpel, and what is formed in the carpel is essentially the male element from the cosmos. The fire spirits are really the messengers, interpreters and implementers of all that rays down into the plant world through the heat of the sun's rays. Working closely with the sylphs, they bring the universal wisdom of the formative forces to bear upon the earth through their living warmth and light, thus ensuring continuity of life on this planet.

Our primary source of heat is, of course, the Sun. It is in a constant state of fluctuation and change, and the fire spirits are programmed to absorb and implement a vast range of solar data entering into our atmosphere on its rays. Sunspots and solar flares have a direct and powerful effect on the magnetic field of the Earth, and this in turn affects everything from the proper functioning of a human brain to the growth of algae. The theory proposing a correlation between solar sunspot cycles and fertility is a compelling one. The Sun's radiation affects the generative processes on Earth via its magnetic field, and during phases of perturbed solar activity this field can influence the body's ability to manufacture melatonin, oestrogen and progesterone. The incoming rays impact on the electromagnetic field emanating from and grounded by our physical body, which in turn influences the progressive balancing of the hormonal phases. From an etheric perspective, this interaction is seen as a spiralling dance of checks and balances between the fire spirits in the warmth ether, the sylphs in the light ether and the undines in the chemical ether.

As we contemplate the element of fire at the hub of procreation, we will eventually come to an understanding that no creature or plant could perpetuate and reproduce on Earth without the activity of the fire spirits. Indeed, no generative increase would be possible without the intricate cooperation of *all* four of the elements and their elementals. As the cycle of the seasons advances and autumn approaches, the fire and root spirits begin to engage in the true dance of fructification within the secret world of plants. In the fecund, nurturing loam of the Earth's topsoil, there is the meeting of male and female elements. The dance of procreation unfolds as follows. From above downwards, the sylph-worked light, or biophotonic activity, is made to leave its imprint within and around the growing plant and, once established there, the 'ideal form' begins to cohere in the ether. During the autumn, this ideal form, or etheric blueprint, descends into the soil and is taken up by the root spirits within the maternal womb of the earth. Meanwhile at the head of the plant, the fire spirits dance in whorls of heat and light around the flowers, and concentrate their living warmth ether into the tiny seed points. This living warmth is then sent down to the root spirits, together with the seed, in order that a new generation of plants can arise out of 'fire' and 'life'!

Rudolf Steiner concludes:

There is a complete lack of clarity about the process of fertilization in the plant world. Up there, outside the Earth, nothing by way of fertilisation takes place; the Earth is the mother of the plant world, the heavens the father. This is the case in a quite literal sense. Plant fertilization takes place through the fact that the gnomes take from the fire spirits what the fire spirits have carried into the carpel as concentrated cosmic warmth on the little airships of the anther pollen ... and with the help of what comes from the fire spirits, the gnomes down below instil life into the plant and push it upwards.[68]

The undines foster the chemical ether in the plant, the sylphs the light ether, the fire spirits the warmth ether. And then the fruit of the warmth ether again unites with what is present below as life. Thus plants can only be understood when they are considered in connection with all that is flitting around them full of life and activity. And one only reaches the right interpretation of the most important process in the plant, when one penetrates into these things in a spiritual way.[69]

From the awesome fire spirits inhabiting the active volcanoes on Earth to the blinding forks of lightning ejecting accumulated heat and anger from our atmosphere, and to the fragile glow on a butterfly wing, the Being of Fire is an ancient and awe-inspiring companion. Expressing itself in things both mighty and minute, there is nowhere where it is not ... for everything in our tangible world is densified fire.

Honour the Being of Fire in all things and consciously invite this great Being into your creative endeavours.

Fire Spirits and Human Thought

'All knowledge in the universe already exists, time is simply a release mechanism to determine what and when we are ready to learn.'[70]

Michael C. Markosky

Earlier in the chapter we learnt how the earth spirits, or gnomes, serve as sensory organs of intelligence within the solid forms of Earth, and also how they maintain the physical integrity and gravity of matter in its countless shapes and structures on this planet. While the essential spiritual substance of an earth spirit is related to human intelligence, the spiritual substance of a fire spirit is related to a human thought; it is important to clarify the difference. The gnomes help to develop the thought capacities of the human brain, while the fire spirits are the carriers of world thoughts into human thought life. So let us explore this mystery more deeply.

One of the most fundamental spiritual truths eluding much of humanity today is that *every thought creates form on some level.* Every thought sounds on for spirit ears, and into every thought is enchanted a fire elemental. Rudolf Steiner explains this process in the following way:

> Fire spirits are inwardly related to [man's] thoughts, to everything which proceeds from the organization of the head. But when someone has progressed so far that he can remain completely in waking consciousness, but nevertheless stand in a certain sense outside himself, viewing himself outside as a thinking being, while standing firmly on the earth, then he will become aware how the fire spirits are the element in the world which makes our thought perceptible on the other side. Thus the perceiving of the fire spirits can enable man to *see* himself as a thinker, not merely to *be* the thinker – and as such hatch out thoughts – but to behold how the thoughts run their course.[71]

So, when we are able to rise above the drama of our own thinking and make a conscious choice to observe it with our witnessing consciousness, in the same way one would watch a sequence of events in a film, we are experiencing the work of the fire spirits.

Many of us are in the thrall of a great illusion, and that is the erroneous belief that we *are* our troubled thoughts. We adhere to this belief because we are so firmly held in the grip of their drama. Negative thoughts tend to stream across the inner screen and hijack what you believe is 'you' in the process; the thoughts actually give the idea that they are the thinker and they are in command of the thinking. Often, when we snap out of a prolonged stretch of negative thinking, there is a sudden flash of recognition – we somehow realize that we had allowed ourselves to be nothing more than a vessel for condemnation and resentment. Thoughts are above all separate entities, and into every thought is enchanted a fire spirit. By pondering the question 'Am I a human being having thoughts, or are thoughts thinking me into being?' we are able to put some time and space between ourselves and a negative thought.

Our true self, our 'I AM' essence, exists in a dimension beyond the mind and all its propositions, and if we take the conscious decision to step out of our thought-drama and move up into the neutrality of our witnessing consciousness, or Vipassana as it is called in the East, we can become acquainted with the real identity of our 'I AM' presence, or higher self. By observing the birth and movement of thought itself, we invite the possibility of an early breakthrough on our journey to spiritual maturity and enlightenment. This key step of pivoting our awareness up and away from the mental shadows is intricately bound up with the activity of the fire spirits, and as we come to acknowledge their work in our thinking we can begin to release ourselves from the tyranny of obsessive, negative thought patterns.

So, let us take a closer look at the process taking place between human thoughts and the fire spirits. In order to grasp the concept behind this interchange, we need to picture a horizon of vast thought forms, imaginations and universal ideas, which are alive and interactive in the astral field of the Earth. One could imagine them as great shimmering clouds hovering over each of the Earth's continents, receiving and reciprocating the world views of each people they envelop. Or one could picture them as vast information trade winds, pulsing around the Earth, offering up ideas and inspiration for the whole of humanity. Meanwhile, the work of the fire spirit in this world picture is to become enchanted into the separate thoughts selected or received by a human being from the universal thought-pool. The thought is then reflected onto the mirroring apparatus of the human brain and worked into composite ideas with other previously chosen or received thoughts. The key to a fulfilling thinking life is understanding who or what is selecting or receiving the thoughts. Is it the fragile 'you', conditioned by traumas of the past, allowing and drawing in the carrion thoughts that continue to sabotage your potential? Or is it the practical 'you' thinking through the everyday necessities? Or is it the divine 'YOU', or higher self, drawing you into the hallowed hunting grounds of high vibrational Imagination, Inspiration and Intuition.

Rudolf Steiner explains the supersensible mechanics of thinking in the following way:

> One notices that through his head man is under the illusion that thoughts are enclosed in his skull. But they are only reflected there. Their mirror images are there. What underlies thoughts belongs to the sphere of the fire beings. If one enters this sphere of the fire beings, one not only sees oneself in the thoughts, but one sees the thought content of the world.[72]

Steiner often uses the phrase 'thought corpse' to describe a thought that has been grasped by the human intellect. This phrase indicates that the thought has left the vast, living, fiery realm of universal thought, and has dropped into the bandwidth of human reckoning. As it hits the mirroring apparatus of the human brain it 'dies' or comes to a halt, so to speak. We then take hold of these 'thought corpses' and work our own will and life force into them, initiating endless, creative endeavours born out of a humanly wrought thinking process.

However, what constitutes human wisdom is already interwoven and impressed into the sphere of the Earth; it is up to the individual to form whatever he or she can from the living wisdom available to humanity. To emphasize this point, Rudolf Steiner uses the example of the purported 'human invention' of paper, when of course the wasps have been creating paper in their nests for millions of years. (And in this case, the wasps are intimately linked with the realm of the fire spirits.) By acknowledging and understanding the work of the fire spirits in human thinking, we can begin to interact with the fiery realm of living wisdom in a more conscious way.

Earlier in the chapter we learnt how the work of the salamanders helps to 'minimize' the cosmos into a seed, enabling each plant to embed a picture of the macrocosmos in its microcosmic seed. From the description of the astral-etheric realm of thought mentioned above, it also appears that they help to 'minimize' the great fiery realm of thought into individual thoughts.

There is always an additional presence behind human endeavour, debate and discussion when the element of fire is included. To light a candle before a meeting or ritual, to exchange ideas and inspiration around a bonfire, or to converse around the blaze of a winter hearth is to include the primal fiery substance of thought itself. The spirits of fire are forever being enchanted into the heat of creative human thinking and inspiration. They know that after countless enchantments and releases they will be taken up by the spiritual glances of the higher hierarchies and return to their spiritual home in the fire mantle of the Earth – and in doing so they carry with them an intimate knowledge of humanity's striving on the mental plane. Contemplating such things gives rise to the question 'Is the thought I am thinking really worthy of a sala-mander's sacrifice?'

Rudolf Steiner's cornerstone book *Knowledge of the Higher Worlds* offers effective and practical exercises for the improve-ment of our thinking life. These exercises help to dismantle nega-tive patterns of thought, improve memory and awaken dormant faculties of cognition and seership. Another recommended title is *Time-Light* by Bryan Hubbard.[73] In this excellent book, the author offers some inspiring and insightful advice on how to deconstruct negative patterns of thinking. He reveals how the past is not just a collection of memories, but a palpable and energetic force that creates structured patterns in our life; it is an entity within us that repeats cycles of events in order to understand itself, and when we recognize this entity, or fire spirit, selectively piloting our memories we can begin to re-contextualize the past and eventually become time-light.

*   *   *

A message from the spirits of fire

Above my home in the hills there is a rocky escarpment that weaves like the spine of a dragon up to a trig point looking out towards Cader Idris.[74] Along this spine is a large rock which seems to rise from the grassland like a whale rising from the ocean, and carved into the whale rock is a perfect seat and vantage point from which to observe the course of the setting Sun as it travels across the hills and plantations from winter to summer solstice. I know each curve and tree along the skyline intimately, since I have become a pilgrim on the yearly path of the Sun. I look forward every year to seeing how its journey through the degrees begins to slow down towards the great pause, the great in-breath, of winter solstice. And then, six months later, on summer solstice eve, I watch a seemingly never-ending sunset, in which the Sun beguiles me into believing it will overturn the laws of earthly motion and sail beyond the north-west ridges of Snowdonia.

Partnering the Sun in this way has given me an entry into the world of fire spirits and the following recollection underlines the profound generosity I have received from them.

Sitting on the whale rock one evening in August, I found myself entering a deep trance of profound gratitude. As I watched the great yellow Sun slowly descending the sky I became acutely aware of the vast River of Life flowing from the Sun into the Earth. Beside me the tall wild grasses were gently swaying in the warm summer breeze, their heads heavy with ripening seeds. I then entered the familiar sensation of time out of time. The devas of the grasses were inviting me to watch them as they leaned towards the Sun. As they swayed in unison towards the westering Sun, every seed in my line of vision lit up into a brilliant, fiery jewel. The fire elementals were revealing themselves to me in the seeds, they were showing me their connection with the will of the Sun – they appeared as minute offspring of the Sun. Every tree in the plantation of spruce and birch, every rock on the escarpment and every head of grass in my sphere of vision was exhorting me to observe how they were graciously sustained by the fire elementals on the River of Life streaming from the Sun. There was no judgement of my previous ignorance or past clumsiness, just a tender and graceful revealing of their domain, and the deeds of the fire spirits within it. I felt honoured and grateful, but I also felt humbled by the fire spirits – the magnitude of their generous sacrifice and their almost intolerable longing to return through the gateway of the Sun to the domain from which they were born sent a profound shudder through my chest. I sent out a pulse of gratitude in response to this gracious revelation, and in return I was held in a shimmering state of presence for a while.

When the heightened sense of presence receded, a message came to me on the River of Life streaming from the Sun, and the devas of the grasses, trees and rocks bore witness to this message. It said: 'Human, call back your scattered fire seeds!'

This was an exhortation to gather the fractured shards of my soul and return them to the living fire of my human heart.

The wisdom of soul-retrieval has long been a staple practice in the shamanic traditions, and the word shaman in the Siberian tongue means 'one who sees in the dark'. In shamanic lore, it is believed that whenever a human experiences an emotional or physical trauma, a fragment of the soul or spirit flees the body in order to survive the experience and, as such, it becomes trapped in limbo. Since receiving the message from the fire spirits of the Sun and the seeds, I have put renewed effort into mining the memories and incidents of my past which have caused the most disruption in the present. If the memory lives in my early years, I address the younger self in the following way:

'Come child, return to the fold. You have abided in this memory long enough, we have a life to live and a world to create. Soul seed, I welcome you back into present time, and into the loving fire of a human heart!'

If it is a more recent memory, I replace the salutation 'Come child' with 'Come friend'.

If you choose to try this exercise yourself, remember that some memories are hard to find and face, and they will need several attempts at soul retrieval. However, you will instinctively know when you have succeeded in the retrieval, because there is a great surge of joy as the fire spirits are released from the long-held thought form around the memor . When you feel the effect of this release, give thanks to all concerned in the memory, and to all concerned with its release. As you free yourself from the emotional charge of personal memory, you begin to see your past as part of a wider cosmic memory. Expanding from personal memory to cosmic memory is an essential step on the path of so l alchemy.

* * *

To our ancient ancestors, the world of elementals and nature spirits was an ever-present, interactive reality. They lived their lives with the spiritual laws of nature deeply ingrained in their tribal consciousness. Up until the decline of the Graeco-Roman period, a human being would look at an object, like a tree, and believe that the essence of the tree itself was being directly transferred into the eye. To be able to see and register an object outside oneself was to receive a direct transference of 'living idea and essence' from the object itself, and this 'living idea and essence' is none other than a focused collective of elementals.

By the ninth and tenth centuries, this cognitive pro ess began to change and follow a new direction. One of the mo t prominent outward expressions of this change surfaced through the Translation Movement of the eighth and ninth centuries, initiated by the Abbasid lineage of Caliphs, who ruled the Islamic world from 750 to 1258. This movement resulted in a great gathering of information and wisdom from around the known world, and it created a bubbling cauldron of scientific potential. Science became a new scholarly discipline, and men like Al Mamoun, Al Razi and Ibn al-Haytham began to develop their methods of scientific observation in order to explain and categorize the visible world around them.

They did this via the use of measurement, analysis and experimentation — experiments that *others* could try, and verify for themselves. They began to organize their knowledge of the material world into specific categories, by applying a systematic approach to their observations. In doing so, a completely new way of comprehending the physical, wrought work of the Earth began to emerge. Their achievements on the physical plane at this point in history mirrored a new pulse on the evolutionary arc of human consciousness, as it moved further away from the old instinctive clairvoyance of our ancient ancestors and descended yet further into earthly matter. Instead of the concept of an 'ideal form and essence' reaching out towards the human being and offering itself up for contemplation, there was a subtle change of direction — the strengthening individual consciousness in humanity was now advancing *towards* the object, armed with a rapidly developing intellect, an increasing ingenuity, and a growing will to categorize and measure the physical phenomena of Earth.

This highly analytical and disciplined observation of the visible world pioneered by the early Islamic scholars is the bedrock on which today's celebrated scientific institutions are built. Yet however brilliant, impressive and respectable the data emanating from these great institutions is, the prevailing models of investigation today are still filtered through a five-sense-only reality. As a result, something as elusive and visceral as the old Aristotelian view of an 'ideal form and essence' informing the human eye is regarded as merely an irrelevant and obsolete philosophical musing. However, for those who are awake and aware at this great time of change, there is a new stream of consciousness entering humanity, and it is beginning to outstrip the old forms of human thinking. A more advanced, multi-sensory and multi-dimensional human being is beginning to emerge, and the truly percipient men and women of science and philosophy will reacquaint themselves with the 'ideal form and essence' in nature and will learn to communicate with it. This will be achieved by understanding the true nature and substance of the human soul and honing its ability to read in the soul substance of the Great Book of Nature.

The new ether sciences are creating a dynamic interface between science and spirit, and we have reached a time when the laboratory must indeed become an altar. At this altar we have an opportunity to consciously address a vast supersensible intelligence and its countless elemental helpers, and to observe how these dynamics respond to our human will and intention. But the potential success of this interface is dependent on our ability to accept the existence of spiritual beings, our willingness to spend periods of meditative union with the supersensible realms of the earth, and on our capacity to practise the fierce moral responsibility that comes with such a union.

Esoteric training in supersensible seership will one day become a staple practice in the scientific curriculum. Like the alchemists of old, our future scientists will once again prepare themselves to observe the enchantment and release of elemental beings in material substance while still retaining a sound intellectual grip on over a thousand years' worth of hard-won scientific data. If this new conversation with the elemental world is then nurtured and developed in an atmosphere of true morality, the results for humanity will be breathtaking. (Dennis Klocek and Dorian Schmidt, who are anthroposophists as well as scientists, have already made good headway along this vital path. Their method-ologies for observing the activity of the etheric and astral dimen-sions are being tried and tested by others, and a new body of supersensible, scientific information is emerging. Further study of their work is highly recommended – see book list on page 163.)

The powerful confluence of quantum physics, bio-technology and computer science is accelerating at an ever-increasing rate. This formidable cross-pollination of ideas and disciplines has already given birth to sophisticated new meta-materials like the carbon nano-tube, and it will soon outstrip the new functional systems like the nano-bot with even more ingenious and ambitious molecular-scale technology. The concept of a 'personal fabricator' that manipulates patterns of atoms and molecules into any object you desire is already being debated. Yet, this ever-increasing mastery over the properties of matter will only really be of use to humanity if it develops in line with a rise in human consciousness. Of what real use is this grand synergy of science if all it does is spawn an even more sophisticated cache of global weaponry, or facilitate even more sinister ways of annihilating human freedom?

At the threshold of the astral-etheric world, the Infinite Divinity and its component parts are only a thought-step away. It is in this hallowed place that the spiritual hierarchies are witnessing the birth of a new being from within humanity – the *Homo spiritus*. This higher aspect of ourselves is seeking entry into our everyday consciousness, and if we allow it to permeate our thinking life it will begin to free our thoughts from their restriction to the head region and open the way for them to arise from an expanded and open heart. To quote Rudolf Steiner:

Hearts are beginning to have thoughts, enthusiasm is no longer generated by obscure mysticism, but by inner clarity supported by thoughts![75]

Elementals in the Human Being

And if a being with eyes organized like those of the present day had looked at the Earth he would not yet have been able to see man... Man was still a spirit being. He floated as a spirit round the Earth and took into himself the finest substances from the environment of the Earth. Then gradually he densified so far that he could descend to where the Earth had already become solid... And man was not born as he is today, but he was so to say, brought forth out of mother earth herself.[76]

Rudolf Steiner

Human beings are the precious offspring of the highest hierarchies and the mother substance of the Earth. As spiritual beings, we have progressed little by little into physical existence. We are on an epic journey from the rarefied heights of spirit, through the depths of matter, and back into the realms from whence we came. In our far, far distant past we and the mother substance were united like a child in amniotic fluid, and the trauma of our protracted split from this rarefied substance lives deep in our collective psyche. At the present time of great awakening we have an opportunity to heal this ancient wound by becoming consciously aware of our ancient esoteric past, and by acknowledging the legions of nature spirits and elementals existing beyond our five-sense-perceptible reality. They represent the mother substance of our age, and they have been evolving alongside us for aeons of time.

The elementals exist within our physical and supersensible bodies. They maintain us with as much industry as they maintain the life cycle of the plant kingdom. They enliven every cell in our body, and enable us to hold our thoughts. With every in-breath, they rush towards us and carry our words on the out-breath. They stream through our bodily fluid and hold us upright within the forces of gravity and levity. Right into the centre of our bones, into the very structure of our skeletal system, we feel the crystal-forming power of the elementals. They are forever enchanting and releasing, expanding and contracting. Above all, they are decoding from and responding to the supersensory information they absorb from the environment. They are the maintenance team for the master-builders of the human form, and our every thought, word and deed is influencing the efficacy of their work. They exist in the food we eat, the water we drink and the air we breathe; they are at work in the heat of our blood and in the fire of our metabolism, and they are the superconductive substance between spirit and form, thought and will, emotion and action. There is nowhere where they are not!

Our apparently solid, physical form is infused with a life-enhancing, focused plurality of elemental beings. This intricate multiplicity of beings woven into a fine filigree of light and life surrounding our human form is called the body elemental or human etheric body. This subtle body is constantly testing the environment around us and asking the question, 'Can I make this a part of me or not?' When we learn to hear the messages from the etheric body, we can become much more discerning about the food we eat and the images we allow into our conscious awareness. The body elemental is the overarching intelligence running the bio-logical mechanisms of our physical body.

The earth, water, air and fire elementals in a human etheric body are in constant interaction with the elementals in our environment. When this knowledge becomes firmly grounded in our thinking, a vital question begins to grow in the imagination: 'Where do I, as a human being, end and the environment begin?' Somewhere in the following statement lies the seed of an answer. 'In the stillness of eternity, I am an indestructible fragment of divinity, yet here on Earth I am an ever-changing pattern of mutual interaction and reciprocity. I am moulded as much by the movement of the distant stars as I am by the hands that touch my face.'

In order to fathom the mystery of mutual reciprocity between ourselves and our surroundings, let us first turn our attention to the world of animals and their relationship with the environment. In his acclaimed book *Anam Cara*, John O'Donohue describes this relationship between Earth and animal in the following way: 'They enjoy a seamless presence, a lyrical unity with the Earth – the knowing of the Earth is in them. They are our ancient brothers and sisters, they already inhabit the eternal.'[77] The intrinsic knowing-ness of the Earth, the uninterrupted connection with the 'mother substance' and the seamless interchange between the plant and animal kingdoms highlights how much we have lost and forgotten in exchange for acquiring our highly competitive, individual intel-lect. Animals have an instinctive connection with the rhythms of Earth and cosmos. This is why they manage to save themselves in times of extreme weather and perilous seismic activity. They have a direct line into a storm's birthing alignment and an earthquake's origin, and it is this direct, conscious bond with the soul of the Earth that we must learn to re-forge. The body of a human being is a highly sensitive instrument; it always knows what is going on around it, but we have forgotten how to listen to and interpret its subtle language.

By permeating our intellect with the pure magic of devoted feelings and profound gratitude, we are able to facilitate the emergence and synaptic changes of neurons in the brain. The neurons become capable of this transformation as a result of our self-willed intent to focus on the positive aspects of life, and in time this process propels us towards a more advanced spiritual awareness and sensitivity. Regular periods spent in meditation and devout contemplation can also generate an increase in grey matter in the brain regions associated with memory, stress and empathy. This leads to an improvement in our ability to manage our emotions and to feel empathy for others. If we consistently raise our thinking into the bandwidth of positive appreciation for the world's great gifts, we have a direct effect on the quality of neuron activity and the thickness of grey matter in the brain.[78] And, of course, by practising appreciation, devotion and meditation we also strengthen and enhance the developing etheric brain or delicate organ of cognition within and beyond the frontal cortex.

6

What Can We Do and How Can We Help?

In this chapter we explore the following topics: the physical effects of negative thought forms; celebrating the rhythms and cycles in nature; preparing ourselves for a meeting with the elemental kingdom.

'Nature itself is pressing us to create connectivity and synergy. Nature is a hierarchy of synergistic convergence – it creates whole new systems at times of crisis.'[79]

Barbara Marx Hubbard

The morphic field, or group soul, of humanity is rapidly changing, and the higher human potential many of us are sensing in this field is urging us on to the next stage of our evolution. The question 'What can I do for the good of all?' is increasingly arising in the collective consciousness, and we are beginning to realize that the only way to ascend to this next stage is to learn how to collaborate in an evolutionary partnership dedicated to the service of all life. On the other hand, there are also many people who feel a sense of paralysis when they face the magnitude of the world's problems. They either retreat into a fantasy world to avoid the raw and fearsome glare of reality or use the reasoning intellect to keep emotion and personal responsibility at bay. But there is always something each and every one of us can do to make a powerful and significant difference to the unfolding destiny of humanity and the Earth, and that is to consciously manage the quality of our own thinking.

From a supersensible point of view, there are no idle thoughts; all thinking produces form on some level. Be it a small disturbance in biophoton activity created by a fleeting moment of anger or a vast thought form created and reinforced over an entire epoch, thought is constantly producing form. We create and mould reality through our conscious intention and every thought has a fractal effect on the collective. We exist in a state of continuous evolution, not in a fixed and permanent tableaux; therefore, our present and future well-being starts with a commitment to an almost warrior-style discipline with regards to our thinking. The dissonance we create in our own mini-sphere when we maintain a regular flow of mental worry, vengeance and resentment shuts down our ability to reach higher levels of consciousness, and it causes sustained wear and tear on our physical organs. In the highly successful best seller *Loving What Is*, by Byron Katie, the author emphasizes again and again how our first priority must be to take responsibility for the interior of our own microcosm, to clean up our own mental environment and to wean ourselves from the addiction of mentally running other people's lives. She wrote: 'Isn't it funny how we're the last place we look? Always trying to change the projected rather than clear the projector.'[80]

By endlessly focusing on the projected, we inhibit ourselves from accessing the inspiration existing at higher levels of consciousness – inspiration that could spark solutions and remedies for many of humanity's problems, including our own. It also prevents us from acquiring the ability to perceive the subtle elemental forces in our environment, and from making a useful contribution to their well-being. A message from the devas of the Findhorn community (in Scotland) through Dorothy Maclean clearly underlines this point when they say: 'The touch of the angels cannot come when you are beset with doubts, burdens and self-limitations. When you are master of yourself and your conditions, you are one of us … and there is a whole dynamic world ready for an intelligent relationship with an aware humanity.'[81]

To consciously participate in the affairs and rhythms of Earth and cosmos must now become a fixed objective for humanity. We can prepare ourselves for this conscious participation by building a sensitive and appreciative relationship with the background generative presence behind the sense-perceptible world. In our recent history we have devalued or trivialized the rituals of the seasons, and as a result we have lost touch with the pulses of universal creation. The more out of rhythm with the Earth we become, the more mentally, emotionally and physically stressed we become. Like our ancient ancestors, we must once more acknowledge and honour the seasonal phases of a year and consciously create rituals for each transition. Celebrating the festivals of the year immediately links us into the universal and planetary rhythms. We also need to take time each day to notice the weather — not just a cursory glance through the window, but an attentive acknowledgement of the manner in which the atmosphere is expressing its mood. Weather is an outward expression of the soul-mood of our planet; it is the soul of humanity and the Earth, imprinting a vision of itself in the elements. There is always an alive, sentient essence within any forceful expression of the weather; when mass, volatile human thinking and emotion coincide with planetary squares and oppositions, they combine to create life conditions for extreme weather to develop. We can all play our part in soothing these life conditions, by remembering to use our witnessing consciousness as much as possible, and by choosing a more measured and compassionate approach when we are faced with tough emotional challenges.

Becoming aware of the phases of the Moon and the angles of the planets is another essential practice if we are to align ourselves with the rhythm of the universe. These alignments have a direct effect on our mental-emotional state, and with forethought we can make useful compensations and adjustments to lessen the disruption caused by challenging transits, and of course maximize the opportunities offered by the more beneficial ones. The living Earth organism is developing within the tableau of the entire galactic system, and humanity too is evolving and advancing within that ever-shifting tableau.

Preparing for Seership

'The inner mood or disposition corresponding to the feelings of sympathy and antipathy must be replaced with what we can call *soul-quiet*, spirit-peacefulness ... an inwardly resolute soul life filled with spirit calm.'[82]

Rudolf Steiner

Before stepping over the threshold into the etheric dimensions of nature, it is of the utmost importance that the forces of a human soul should be strengthened by appropriate preparation. Some of the preparatory exercises and advice offered in the following paragraphs have been inspired by the exercises presented in *Knowledge of the Higher Worlds*. For over a hundred years this classic has been a staple for those wishing to see into the super-sensible realms, and it continues to be a popular choice for any serious student of esoteric knowledge. Reading this important book in conjunction with the information below is highly recommended.

One of Rudolf Steiner's primary edicts for developing an inter-active relationship with the generative presence behind all life is to *find and create a sheath of soul-quiet*. This phrase covers the many prayers, meditations and ceremonies extant in the world's spiritual traditions, which point to a period of preparation and silence before consciously interacting with the supersensible world. Establishing a mood of soul-quiet allows us to hear the language of our soul. It enables us to reach a level of receptivity where we can communicate with the soul of nature itself. There has to be a point of anchorage which we set sail from — and return to. This demarcation point is important in the early stages of supersensible work, until the interaction becomes more methodical and fluid. To find and create a sheath of soul-quiet entails both slowing down the frenetic mental activity commandeering our thinking life and releasing the tension and constraint around the heart area caused by our sympathies and antipathies. Many people immediately resist these first simple requirements. Why? There are three main reasons why, and if spoken aloud they would probably sound like this:

If I slow down, I'll notice my suffering and I won't be able to bear it.
If I open my heart, I will be vulnerable and people will take advantage of me.
If I stray from the edicts of my left-brain, intellectual education, I may invite ridicule and therefore lose my standing in society.

Yet, we have reached a time in earthly evolution when such fears have to be overcome if we are to align with the new human potential arising in our collective consciousness. As many of us endeavour to evolve from *Homo sapiens* to *Homo spiritus*, there is really only one vital work to accomplish — work on ourselves. As more of us take on this vital work, the natural consequence of our progression into the enlightened states will be a healing of the environment around us. And as each of us evolve we change the whole, making it easier for those who follow in our footsteps.

Creating a sheath of soul-quiet is a basic practice in this work. In most spiritual traditions creating the sheath starts with a period of steady rhythmical breathing from the diaphragm and a silent con-templation of the divine 'I Am' essence, or higher self, within. This ancient, divine, all-seeing part of the self will always tell the truth, and it looks out on everything with depth and discernment. It is the bridge-builder, the peacemaker and the pathfinder within you, and it becomes an undeniable, experiential reality when you truly grasp that you are a divine being with a spiritual origin and a spiritual destiny. Developing a regular connection with this mature and compassionate part of yourself and discerning the delicate wisdom emanating from its core is an essential practice on any true spiritual path.

There are many ways to approach this part of yourself. The fol-lowing meditations are just two examples of an approach to the eternal world of the higher self, using the words 'Love' and 'Peace'. The first is taken from *Meditation: Guidance of the Inner Life*[83] by Friedrich Rittelmeyer, and the second, entitled 'The Four Facets', is presented by the author and peace ambassador Isha Judd in her book *Why Walk When You Can Fly?*[84]

The first meditation, by Friedrich Rittelmeyer, unfolds as follows. First gently take in the word 'Peace', or 'I am peace', on the in-breath and begin to release your busy thoughts on the out-breath. After a while the word 'Peace' becomes a physical sensation in the body, and there is a natural progression to a state where you begin to send out the word 'Love', or 'I am love' on the out-breath. The Revd Rittelmeyer advises us to 'Let peace sound out until it dies away into love, so that it can be no selfish and passive peace but the peace that unites itself with the world's evolving.'

Send your love and gratitude out into the immediate environment. This simple inner chant sets up a nurturing, rhythmic exchange. At first it aligns you with the healing rhythm of your own breathing, then it aligns you with the in-breath of night and the out-breath of day. At a later point it will align you with the deep in-breath of winter and the long out-breath of summer, thus bringing you into a grand alignment with the breathing of the Earth herself. In time, this meditation will help you to feel focused and stable enough to seek the guidance of the Christ within or, according to your religious or spiritual belief, address your higher self within. When you have reached a place of stillness, quietly ask for help and guidance on your path, and then say the words 'I am listening'. Listen. Allow yourself to enter into a gracious trance of receptivity, while maintaining a link with your body awareness, and in time you will receive the guidance you need to work with the intelligence of the land. (For further information on the 'I am Peace' meditation see *Meditation: Guidance of the Inner Life* by Friedrich Rittelmeyer, pages 30–3).

The second meditation, 'The Four Facets' by Isha Judd, runs as follows:

'Praise love for this moment in its perfection'
'Thank love for this human experience in its perfection'
'Love creates me in my perfection'
'Om Unity'

While taking your attention into your heart, contemplate each of the four facets, deeply and thoroughly. Take a pause and leave a space between each one. When you contemplate the fourth facet, take your attention to the bottom of your spine and up to the crown of your head – this grounds the entire experience into the core of your body and into the land. After spending time with these gracious phrases, you can reach a place of stillness and peace. In this peaceful state you will be able to discern the guidance from your higher self and hear the messages from the intelligence of the land.

While making contact with your higher self, begin to visualize a sheath of protection around yourself. This can be done by imagining a pure, protective globe of light, or a sphere of shimmering silver, around yourself. Another standard practice is to mentally mark the seven directions of east, south, west and north, the sky above, the earth below, and the spark of divinity within – essentially, creating an octahedron around yourself. In both cases it is advisable to visualize a cord from the base of your spine grounding you into the earth, and a link from the crown of your head connecting you to the sky. Again, it is important to emphasize that nurturing an unshakeable belief in one's own divinity is at the core of all true protection.

The octahedron or globe can also be created from the chamber of the heart. This is done by dropping your attention down into the heart area and envisioning a small vibrant globe or diamond in the centre of your chest. Focus on this radiating shape and begin to expand it out until it completely surrounds you. By working in this way you create and manage an environment with boundaries, which has the potential to limit outside interference and also inhibit your own negative thoughts from impacting the immediate surroundings. It creates a framed space, or mini-sphere, in which we can improve and refine our own personal energetic field. This is the anchorage point, the point of demarcation, and the quality of resonance within this mini-sphere will, in time, affect the macro-sphere in a positive and useful way. Once you have completed this visualization, let it be, and move on to the next stage.

The sheath of soul-quiet is an essential garment on the path to seership. With patience and practice it will allow you to enter a steady and receptive mood with increasing ease. The sheath is clearly visible to the inhabitants of the spiritual world, and it indicates that you are potentially willing to communicate. In time, you will begin to sense that you are not alone with your thoughts and emotions — a feeling that other beings are gazing into your consciousness will become apparent. And every attempt at soul-quiet, devout contemplation, focused prayer and deep gratitude will help you to develop a sense of community with these invisible and helpful observers.

The nature spirits are especially responsive to our feelings, and they clearly perceive how our feelings impact on the environment. We need to understand the true nature and substance of human feeling if we wish to communicate with them. The following exercise is designed to help you observe, balance and educate your feelings. First, find and create your sheath of soul-quiet. Build an atmosphere of quiet composure around yourself. Gently direct your will into the swell of your thoughts, feelings and fears, and begin to still the turbulent waters. When you feel a degree of balance and poise, begin to contemplate the word 'joy'. Bring to mind joyful memories, thoughts and imaginations and allow them to propel you into a strong feeling of joy. Let it grow and envelop you. When you feel the full expansion and sensation of joy, drop all the memories and thoughts, and focus on the feeling itself. Observe it, memorize it, explore its substance thoroughly. Ask the questions 'What is joy doing with me in this moment?' and 'What is my relationship to this feeling?' Make a note of the colours, gestures and sensations experienced in the exercise, and then repeat it using the word 'sorrow'. Endeavour to work through the powerful sensation of sorrow with composure and equanimity.

By honing our ability to observe the highly mobile substance of feeling with our witnessing consciousness, we can strengthen the spiritual muscle needed to make a sensitive feeling-analysis of the ether. The nature spirits communicate with a wide palate of feelings, therefore we need to understand the 'linguistics' of feeling if we wish to converse with them. (For further details on the 'Joy and Sorrow' exercise, and other exercises designed to balance the feeling life, see *Six Steps to Self-Development* by Rudolf Steiner.[85])

The first steps towards a serene soul disposition take courage, commitment and a knowingness that our own innate divinity and guidance system, if properly approached and nurtured, will lead us into a new bandwidth of understanding — one that will allow us to see the *content* of our life in a new and expanded *context*. A key step towards developing a strong anchorage point in the ever-shifting tableau of the astral-etheric world is a commitment to mental, emotional and physical morality, and an unwavering self-honesty.

The journey from a plinth of self-delusion to the grounded relief of self-honesty has always provided a good template for fiction and drama, because we instinctively recognize this tug of war within ourselves. Great novelists like Jane Austen and George Eliot nearly always mined their most insightful observations from the mayhem caused by self-delusion. In her timeless classic *Emma*, Austen points out how 'seldom, very seldom does complete truth belong to any human disclosure',[86] and indeed, within the minefield of human relationships, we have become adept at hiding our true nature from ourselves and others. However, truthful disclosure to oneself is a mandatory requirement in spiritual work, if we are ever to forge a meaningful relationship with the living wisdom in nature and the spark of divinity within ourselves and others. Pride and dishonesty create a repellent cloud on the astral-etheric planes. We must not be deceived by our own wishes, and we need to acknowledge the truth that there is no such thing as a private thought – every thought, word and deed sounds on for spirit ears and eyes, and every thought rebounds on us for better or for worse.

Rudolf Steiner warns us that lies devour the soul, and he also impresses on us the need to guard and control our thoughts when we cross the threshold into the supersensible realms. Our thoughts are more easily recognized as separate entities, with force fields of their own, when we observe them in these realms. Hatred, conceit, arrogance and complaining send out a strong field of chaotic dissonance, which instantly perturbs and imprints itself in the ether. Negative thoughts and beliefs are energetic fields that distort reality and cause it to shudder and shake into disorder. Endless self-berating also creates an unpleasant dissonance, and is in fact a highly destructive and corrosive indulgence. John O'Donohue expresses this point so clearly when he says, 'The judgemental eye is always equally harsh with itself. It only sees the images of its tormented interiority projected outwards from itself. The judgemental eye harvests the reflected surface and calls it truth. It enjoys neither the forgiveness nor imagination to see deeper into the ground of things where truth is paradox.' When we commit ourselves to a curtailment of this particular indulgence, one of the early positive results is an improvement in the quality of our dreams. We have a moral and spiritual responsibility to find and recognize our own worthiness, because to be a perpetual gloomy guest on Earth is to be a burden to nature. And it would be well to remember that choosing between a cheerful or a morose attitude can bring about forces of liberation or imprisonment for our friends in the elemental kingdom.

The elemental kingdom will remain elusive and out of reach until we take responsibility for our own emotional maturity.

Yet we are human, and our emotional systems are more powerful than our minds – reason and passion are forever jousting for supremacy. Our potent sympathies and antipathies draw us into a relentless cycle of events which challenge and mould us. They trigger living currents, sensations and thought forms within us, which can either jolt us into a bright new landscape of understanding or rob us of the energy needed to make a profound and life-changing connection with the spiritual dimensions in nature, and open relationships with other human beings. A systematic management of the more destructive thought forms in our daily lives is the key, and a particularly effective practice to follow is where you gather your troublesome thoughts together and make a 'deed of surrender'. In a traditionally western style, such a surrender would sound something like this:

> 'I offer up these thoughts to thee O Lord, that they may be transformed by Thy Grace and returned to me as useful thoughts and deeds.'
> (The words 'O Lord' and 'Grace' can be replaced with a phrase or word that aligns with your own particular spiritual tradition.)

This petition can also be sent *into* the Earth, calling on Gaia to absorb and transform the negativity. There is an astral-etheric dimension within the Earth that is readily able to assimilate and transmute such uneasy offerings. But for an offering such as this to be transformed efficiently it has to be surrounded and directed with proper intent. (It is important to note that there is a significant difference between the uncontrolled 'thought junk' of the gloomy guest and the 'uneasy offerings' of a spiritual student who consciously asks for help.)

You can also carry this surrender through into a physical act, like placing your head against a cool rock face or a stout and healthy tree and then asking for help to transform your troublesome thoughts. After a while, you will feel what can only be described as a 'subtle fomentation' taking place, as the elementals endeavour to tranquillize some of your thoughts and draw them into the earth. If you decide to try this particular practice, always remember to seek permission first. You do this by addressing the tree, boulder, etc., either mentally or by the spoken word, and then hold a focused, steady vision of what you wish to do. The elementals and nature spirits are then able to read the astral-etheric picture of your request and will either respond with a sense of welcoming or they will simply be neutral. When you feel sure of the welcome or neutrality, proceed with a deed of surrender. In the unlikely event that you feel a resistance, respectfully end the communion and move to another tree, boulder or location until you feel a channel is open and responsive. *Always* give your heartfelt thanks to the elementals of the location, and leave an offering in the form of a prayer, a song or a sprinkling of food afterwards.

The impulse behind this deed of surrender, whether it is sent upwards into the heavens or downwards into the earth, is an acknowledgement that something higher than our human intellect is needed to successfully out-smart the compulsive and addictive nature of entrenched negative or chaotic thinking. We have to allow the divinity within us and around us to inspire a new context for the troublesome content of our lives.

Another gracious, powerful and effective phrase to contemplate and practise is the following phrase adapted from the 'Act of Con-secration of Man'[87] brought to us by Rudolf Steiner. It is intended to limit the effect our negative thoughts and words have on our fellow human beings and on our immediate environment.

'Before me, may the threshold be guarded, a wall hinder my error from streaming around me, all evil be taken from my words [thoughts and deeds], and goodwill pour into them...'

Then say, 'I ask this with grace, and I ask this for the good of all.'

With regular use, these phrases create a very real and effective structure in the supersensible field around us.

By consciously surrounding, gathering and offering up your thoughts using the methods described above, you lessen the damage your woes and resentments do to the supersensible environment around you and to the elementals existing within you, and by doing so the fragile window into the etheric world can stay open. Impatience with, and hard resistance to, these arising uneasy thought forms only increases their ability to hijack your internal mental screen. So another helpful phrase to use when you wish to enter quiet contemplation but feel ambushed by your thinking is to address the thoughts themselves, saying: 'I acknowledge you, but leave me now, and I will attend you later.' By doing this, there is no hard angle of denial or suppression.

Along with preparing the inner mental screen for a connection with the living presence in nature, we also need to take note of our bodily sensations and physical well-being. In his excellent booklet *Observations in the Field of Formative Forces in Nature*,[88] the highly skilled seer Dorian Schmidt tells us how to recognize two extremes in our physical state. He says, 'If [our] forces are too weak, for instance through fatigue or "drying up" after one-sided head work, or after spending a long time in places which are overloaded with electrical effects, then the living streams, the ones that we really want to experience, flow past our consciousness and can only help us to regenerate our bodies. And if one day we leap out of bed in the morning, bursting with energy and with the feeling we could uproot trees, we will only be able to perceive our own bodily nature.'

By seeking the middle path between these two extremes, we will come to find the physical poise needed to perceive the formative, etheric activity around us.

Creating and reinforcing a dedicated space in which to work with our witnessing consciousness is, and always has been, the key to a successful spiritual practice. Within this protected free space, we are able to recognize and dismantle the negative, limiting 'programs' running our thinking and feeling life. Classic thought forms like 'I am not worthy', 'The world is a fearful place', 'There is not enough' and 'I must suffer greatly in order to gain' are a few of the most powerful programs running many people's lives today. Each established thought form behaves like a vortex. Its strong suctional force draws similar thoughts, memories and ideas unto itself in order to reinforce and perpetuate its very existence. Many of us see life filtered through these powerful programs because they have been accepted and unchallenged for generations through our hereditary lines. It is of great importance to recognize how these programs unconsciously influence the course of our life. When we begin to understand their supersensible nature, and we bring our witnessing consciousness to bear upon them, they will start to disintegrate and slowly dismantle. And by doing so the legions of fire spirits enchanted into these forms will be released, thus freeing vast amounts of trapped energy which can then be joyously recycled into more positive programs and endeavours.

*   *   *

In the following recollection, I give an example of a powerful message from the angelic realm, conveyed through the nature spirit of a great oak tree.

Recently, I attended a gathering of like-minded souls at the beautiful location of Hawkwood College[89] in Gloucestershire. I had come to learn the techniques of seership, presented by the anthroposophist Dorian Schmidt, mentioned earlier in this chapter. Over the last twelve years, Dorian has developed his own unique methodology of research into the life forces working behind physical matter, and he has inspired many people to make their own explorations into the world of formative forces.

On the second day of the seminar, we gathered in a field. In the middle of this field was a large, four-hundred-year-old oak tree. Our task was to walk from the edge of the field towards the tree and to sense where the aura of the tree began. After sensing the aura, we were asked to slowly walk towards the tree and to gather as much supersensible information as we could from the nature spirit of the tree. As the group walked towards the tree, we all seemed to sense the aura at the same distance from the tree. After I had felt the aura, I was unable to face the tree for a while. Why? Because I sensed that whatever the tree was about to convey to me was so powerful I would need some sort of preparation before receiving its message. I kept my eyes upon the ground, cleared my head of all untidy 'thought-junk' and began to breath deeply. After about a minute I raised my eyes to the tree ... and received one of the most powerful downloads from the elemental kingdom I have yet experienced. The gift was instantaneous, its wisdom universal, its application essential – the message entered the very core of my being and resounded with the words:

'HUMAN, REVERENCE THYSELF!'

The great wisdom in these three words exhorts us to find and recognize our worthiness and holiness, and it points to the root of most of humanity's problems. When we truly grasp the mystery of who we are – divine-spiritual beings having an earthly experience in a biological life form – there is no choice but to reverence all life, and the fastest route to that essential knowingness is to first 'reverence thyself'. The seemingly ceaseless war created by our inner voices and the relentless loop of self-judgement and recrimination that so many of us find ourselves locked into simply cannot withstand the holy light and resonance of a declaration like 'Human, reverence thyself!' Declare these words to yourself and see what happens to your inner life.

I believe this declaration came from the archangelic realm. The great beings of this realm use the more robust nature spirits of the earthly realm to be their emissaries. One only has to look into an ancient text like the Old Testament to see how angelic encounters were received with the utmost dread – a far cry from the rather sentimental expression of the angels favoured by the retail markets of today. Apart from a select few, most human beings would not be able to survive a direct encounter with the angelic hierarchies – it would almost certainly blow the circuits of our nervous system. These great beings are increasingly exhorting us to wake up at this perilous time in our history, and they are using the nature spirits to convey their essential and timely wisdom into the human kingdom.

This message of reverence continues to bring me waves of wisdom and realization in its wake, and I believe it will continue to do so for many *years to come. I am profoundly grateful and deeply appreciative of this auspicious gift.*

After I had received this gracious message, I walked towards the tree and found myself crossing a threshold into the shimmering, mobile, etheric world of the oak. I could clearly see how the earth spirits, or gnomes, were holding the trunk of this mighty tree in place. They were tucked in tightly together like little brown birds within the bark, and they were constantly receiving and upholding the song of creation filtering through the overarching Spirit of Oak.

The poignancy of their love and sacrifice was shattering.

The bitter must be experienced as well as the sweet. And after a heightened experience such as this there is nearly always a period of solemnity. A sensation of the stress endured by the elemental kingdom, due to humanity's relentless vandalism of the environment, resonated through me at an almost intolerable volume for a while. However, this poignant revelation only served to underline more deeply the profound wisdom of the directive to 'Reverence thyself'. By reverencing the self, the holy path from ignorance to wisdom, and thoughtlessness to mindfulness, shines ever more brightly before the mind's eye.

Unconditionally reverencing the self may seem an impossible task at times, and yet it is a precious gift we can give to the Earth. When we learn to reverence the self, everything begins to flow in our external world. It is the responsibility of every human being to come home to their divine essence and greatness and, in turn, emanate that greatness into the community around them.

7

Making Contact

We will now explore the following practices: how to deepen your connection with the living intelligence of the land, and how to hone your ability to observe the shimmering phenomena existing in the etheric field of the Earth.

In the previous chapter we explored the mental, emotional and physical requirements needed to enhance our own sensitivity and receptivity, and we looked at ways in which we could prepare ourselves for contact with the inhabitants of the ether. The next step along the way is to find a location of great natural beauty, or one where the nature forces are strong and healthy. Choose a place where you will not be disturbed. Make yourself comfortable. Remember to take warm clothing with you, as the sensation of shivering will only pull your attention into your physical discomfort and away from the finer sensations you will need to discern during the meditation.

When you are ready, begin to build and create a sheath of soul quiet around yourself and follow the meditation procedure described in the previous chapter on page 110. After a while imagine you are dropping a grounding chord from the base of your spine into the bedrock of the earth, and imagine a connection from the crown of your head to the sky above. Then breathe rhythmically from the diaphragm for a while. Become aware of your entire body, including your back, your crown and the soles of your feet — remember your body is a sensitive barometer. With your eyes closed take your attention to the area at the back of your eyes where your pineal gland[90] is situated. Enter into quiet communion with the silence inside yourself. Be still and attentive and quietly greet yourself — greet that indestructible part of yourself which can discern an authentic supersensible experience from a moment of fantasy, that non-local aspect of yourself called the 'divine higher self'. Ask that your discernment be clear and precise. Make this request with grace and ask that it be for the good of all. After a while, gently tap your sternum and feel the chamber of your heart begin to thrum.

It is advisable to have your eyes closed when you begin this practice and then open them at a later point – you will instinctively feel when it is appropriate to do so. As you become more experienced and familiar with the supersensible nature of your chosen location, you may wish to keep your eyes open in soft-focus throughout your meditative preparation. If you are unexpectedly disturbed during your meditation, step yourself across a bridge into normal responsive awareness by breathing evenly and counting to five; this will save you from jolting your astral-etheric body unnecessarily.

There will probably be waves of resistance and emotional discomfort when you begin your meditation, as every experienced meditator will testify. But after a while the discomfort begins to turn into something familiar – like an old cumbersome piece of furniture that you have been meaning to recycle for ages. And if you persevere and stay with the process, you will begin to experience periods of breakthrough into a state of heightened awareness and attentiveness; these will begin to lengthen as you become more adept. Humming, overtoning or repeating a mantra like 'I and the environment are one' can help you to reach a quiet soul-mood of receptivity – and the more you slow down and escort your unwanted thoughts out on your breath, the longer the breakthroughs of attentive awareness will become. At the threshold between sound and silence we can begin to hone our skill of truly listening. To truly listen is a deed of worship and devotion, and when we learn to listen to the Earth with our souls we come into unity with the rhythm and song of Creation.

The sounds in nature, like the breeze, the birds, the insects and the grazing animals, will begin to resonate at a different amplitude on the background silence. They appear to sound like players in a vast orchestra. You can merge with this orchestra by gently singing the vowels in long, quiet tones for a few minutes. Every sound and every gesture from the animal, insect and plant world will then take on a new significance and meaning. They become messengers and guides, and you may feel an impulse to follow the narrative these gestures suggest. While you enter into resonance with your environment in this way, allow your eyes to go 'soft'. In other words, do not strain every nerve to 'see something' but allow your vision to become gentle and all inclusive. It is at this point that the interaction with your environment can truly begin, and you can feel yourself to be a fellow musician in the orchestra. During this process, greet and say 'hello' to the living, generative presence in your surroundings and then wait; over time you will begin to feel the subtle sense of a return greeting. While opening to the possibility of a response, it is helpful to contemplate a particularly poignant and powerful phrase by Rudolf Steiner, a phrase that can help you to truly fathom the deep mysteries working behind nature. It is simply this:

Yielding to beauty brings forth 'a pious devotion to infinity'.[91]

The consequences of such a yielding or surrender into beauty are described as follows:

A person who does not merely stare but ponders over nature, a person who feels the beauty of things ennobles his impressions — what does such a person do? As a result of his spiritual activity, he redeems the elemental being that streams towards him from the outer world, thus raising it to its previous state. He releases the elemental being from its enchantment.

In this passage, Dr Steiner shows us how, through our deep contemplation and profound appreciation of nature, we can release elemental beings who are enchanted into form, and by doing so we help them on their return path to the rarefied dimensions from whence they came. *This is a devout deed of service to the Earth and her elementals that each and every one of us can perform almost anywhere at any time.*

A comparative analogy with this surrender into beauty is to imagine you are a crystal of salt, slowly dissolving into water. Eventually, when you become familiar with the practice of yielding, or dissolving, into your surroundings, the delineation between you and nature begins to soften and you become one with your environment. There is a distinct feeling that you have become more porous and your senses have become more mobile. Ensure you do not lose your sense of consciousness during this process, and in the beginning only try this visionary meditation for short periods, taking care each time to 'reassemble' yourself and return to your centre. Your task here, is to summon the courage to dissolve and free-fall into a profound wave of appreciation and gratitude, and to allow this wave to permeate everything around you. Appreciation is the essential substrate in which we must work; it is a fertile soil in which to sow the seeds of supersensible perception. In the following quotation Rudolf Steiner underlines the need to adapt ourselves to very different rules and conditions when we cross the threshold into the elemental world. It is a world of mobility, metamorphosis and transformation, and there is no permanent, enclosed, circum-scribed form as we know it in the physical sense world:

> In the elemental world we get to know another being only when in a way we inwardly 'become' the other. When we have crossed the threshold, we have to move through the elemental world in such a way that with every step we transform ourselves into every single happening, creep into every being ... the threshold that sharply divides the sense world from the supersensible world must be respected absolutely; the soul must observe the requirements of each of the two worlds, adapting and conducting itself differently on this side and that.[92]

The Old Testament teaching proclaiming human dominion over

the kingdoms of the Earth has been misinterpreted for too long, and it has had disastrous consequences for humanity and the environment. However, the most effective way to dismantle this mighty thought form is to regularly commit yourself to entering a meditative state of profound love and appreciation for the Earth's great gifts. As you yield yourself into a wave of appreciation, you will begin to feel a thrumming and an expansion in the heart area. Try not to resist this sense of expansion; summon the courage to allow the bands of restriction around your heart to loosen. Many people baulk at this sensation of expansion in the early stages, because it can ignite a very personal fear — a fear that one is going to be unalterably changed by the experience. Here again, we need to bring our witnessing consciousness into play to track these fears, until they too loosen and re-emerge metamorphosed into new ways of comprehending our reality.

With perseverance and courage, the subtle layers of wisdom embedded in nature will slowly begin to reveal themselves as your consciousness expands. A natural extension of your normal perceptive capabilities will begin to develop, and with an enhanced visual acuity you will begin to decode the more subtle information embedded in the higher dimensions of reality. The etheric realms, which are usually excluded from your normal range of perception, will begin to open up and be integrated into your conscious awareness. The authenticity of these revelations can be verified by a very particular feeling, best described in the following statement: 'Of course I know this, I've known it all along, I'd just forgotten!' Therefore let us call this key, fundamental feeling, this warm rush of understanding *The Remembrance*, and whenever this feeling arises, you will know that you have hit a pocket of supersensible truth in your sensory awareness.

For many people, the idea of using one's gut feeling is not a new one, but to meticulously read and track one's feelings and use them as the primary antennae in a situation is probably a new experience. Initially the solar plexus and the heart, rather than the head, take the primary position of discernment – they act like a radar. Unfamiliar as this practice may seem at first, it is the wide-ranging feeling sensations that eventually enable you to discern the fluctuating frequencies beyond the sense-perceptible world. The human body is a great barometer, and in the early stages of this work, when you begin to receive a feeling response, try not to pounce on it, label it and fire a quiver full of intellectual arrows at it. Just mentally stand back and let the feeling truly unroll itself, and link to others if needs be, before applying a mental interpretation. The intellect always wants to keep control and 'pilot the vehicle' at all times, but we have to learn to bridle it when we do this work. It will, however, be richly rewarded in time, because the strong waves of experiential knowingness that enter our life during the process of seership ultimately relieve the intellect of doubt. An intellect with less doubt to process is a leaner, cleaner instrument to carry on the path towards enlightenment.

The president of the Hagia Chora School for Geomancy in Germany, Marko Pogacnik, is an advanced seer and a skilled interpreter of the elemental kingdom. He states: 'Nature Spirits do not understand our thoughts in words, but rather read our messages from the feeling vibrations which accompany the spoken words. They think the way we feel.'[93] He describes how he receives a response from the elementals in the following way: 'I receive the response in a kind of mysterious mixture of projected images and inspired thoughts which I try simultaneously to decipher in a state of attentive meditation ... in conversations with the elementals [they] answer with a cloud of feelings which I translate into logical sentences.'[94]

Viewed from the witnessing consciousness, our mental constructs and meticulous labelling have their uses but, more often than not, they can actually separate us from life. By yielding to beauty and the exquisite aliveness in nature, we can become aligned once more with a profound and encompassing love that underlies all-that-is. In the following quotation Dorothy Maclean introduces us to a view of this love from the point of view of the nature spirits:

> It is said that the devic realm has no love and it is true that we do not have the limited, preferential love that humans have, we simply live in love like fish in water. You isolate love, you pick and choose whom to love; our realm is a sea of love, for our hearts speak to the greatest love of all, Love itself, and our energies go out to all worlds. We could not blend our consciousness if our love was limited. One becomes one with what one loves and this is apparent everywhere ... when you love only your limited self you are alone, we know no aloneness ... You will become more and more aware of the sea of love in which we all live, in which we all partake. At present you find a thousand things to block your awareness of it, but nevertheless you live in it ... as you touch more deeply into this life you will experience this love.[95]

With dedication and perseverance, we can all begin to touch and tap into what the devas call 'The Sea of Love', and an early response to such perseverance is a heightened perception of the workings of the ether. One of the first phenomena many people see is the delicate, scintillating whorls of life spinning around the flowers and trees. These are best observed on sunny days. The surest way of knowing that you are witnessing an authentic etheric field around a plant is the realization that it makes no difference to your view of the phenomena whether you wear glasses or not – the image is the same. Although it is constantly shimmering, the clarity of outline is identical with or without glasses, because something beyond ordinary sight is also registering these shimmering whorls. It is an awakened extension of our normal vision, a kind of super-sight. Each species of flower and tree has a unique pattern in its etheric field, and once you have awakened your super-sight you will be able to observe this shimmering preparatory field around the material foliage. These sparkling whorls are life itself, and they sustain and uphold the entire plant kingdom of the Earth.

Tree Meditation

The following simple meditation will help you to see the etheric whorls of light around plants, and nurture your ability to feel a response from the nature spirits. First, find a quiet location where the plant life is strong and healthy, then choose a tree to work with. Walk towards your chosen tree and stop at a point where you can easily behold the entire shape of the tree in your line of vision. Nod, smile or whisper a greeting to the tree. Then sit on the ground and begin to truly absorb the outline and gesture of the tree. Use your imagination to trace the biography of the tree from its birth out of a seed to its fully formed expression in present time. Observe every nuance, gesture and colour in its trunk, branches and leaves, and observe the shimmering air around its canopy. Yield yourself into a trance of exploration, and allow this trance to evolve into an act of prayerful wonder and deep gratitude for the tree.

Then, after a while, gently cease your exploration and move into a state of poised receptivity, and let the tree know you would welcome a response. Wait. If the conditions are right and the energetic connection between you and the tree is in place, you will begin to feel a gesture of response birthing itself from the centre of the tree. Be still and attentive and allow this gesture to extend itself to you, and allow it to have an *effect* on you. Let the gesture and effect run its course without trying to mentally decipher them; when you are ready, walk up to the tree and give respectful thanks for the communication. Allow this exchange to fully sink in and leave some space and time before subjecting it to a detailed mental investigation.

The more you practise this exercise, the more receptive you will become to the subtle energetic field of the ether and, as a result, the whorls of light around the tree will become more discernible. If you live in the northern hemisphere, it is best to try this exercise in sunlight during the months of April, May and June when the foliage-forming forces are at their most active.

* * *

As you become more experienced in your meditations and more receptive to the fine nuances emanating from the land, you will begin to slip into the heightened, intuitive state needed for super-sensory perception with increasing ease. The transition from the temporal world to the fringes of the eternal world will become less ritualized and more spontaneous as your sheath of soul-quiet drops into place more rapidly, and the messaging between your higher self and the intelligence of the land will become more fluid.

Colour Waves

Among the phenomena often observed in the early stages of supersensible perception, are waves of shimmering colour hovering close to the Earth's surface. These are waves of pure, living colour working freely in the atmosphere between the sense and super-sensible realms. Our experience of colour is usually limited to observing it as a constituent part of a physical object, for example the red of a tomato, the green of a leaf and the blue of a cornflower. But colour is a supersensitive, living substrate that weaves in and out of form, and each colour in the spectrum conjures a different soul-mood.

The colour waves are best seen in wild places untouched by human agriculture, for example they can be seen over mountain lakes and tarns, or wild pasture land (see description of water spirit on page 72). They have a similar appearance to the Aurora Borealis, although they hover over a specific area rather than pulsing in multicoloured waves. They are most active in the spring and summer when the Earth breathes out her elementals. The elementals, and especially the sylphs, make use of this substrate of living colour as they blossom into activity in the spring. For the budding seers who are beginning to acquire a wider visual acuity, it is always a deep joy to observe these waves hovering over the late spring landscape for the first time.

* * *

My experiences with supersensible colour have been many and varied. The colour waves I see most often are the extensive bands of translucent colour hovering over the high pasture land of mid-Wales in late spring. It is a moving and joyful sight, and I always feel privileged to be allowed into this dimension of living, vibrating colour. I am also able to see small, intensive, flame-shaped colours emerging from the earth, especially in places of geomantic potency. I particularly remember seeing vibrant examples of this phenomenon emerging from the earth around the Michael and Mary stones of Avebury. The colour flames were approximately six to ten inches high and they radiated in intense shades of blue and yellow.

This radiant substrate of supersensible colour can also be harnessed by spiritual beings from Higher Devachan in order that they may become visible to human beings, on the rarefied levels of the physical plane. I remember experiencing this phenomenon during a seminar presented by Lama Gangchen, a much loved Tibetan master and graduate of Sera and Tashi Lhunpo (two of the major monastic universities of Tibet). At this gathering Lama Gangchen taught us methods of self-healing based on the wisdom and mantras of the Blue Medicine Buddha, also known as Sangye MenLa. As the afternoon progressed, I began to see flashes of azure blue in the corner of my eye. By the end of the day, I could see a three-foot-high shimmering shape of intense azure blue, flashing and winking in and out of visible reality behind the Lama. Quite clearly, this was an aspect of the Medicine Buddha manifesting itself in a rarefied colour form, in response to a group of focused human beings gathered in prayer, meditation and song. The authenticity of this visual experience was confirmed not only by hearing it discussed by others in the room, but also by my feeling that powerful homing thought, 'The Remembrance' – that key feeling which says, 'Of course, I remember this, I knew this all along!'

I believe the visual acuity that allowed me to see the Blue Buddha and also the colour flames of Avebury was enhanced by my being part of a group of like-minded souls – a group whose chief intent was to bring about self-healing and an increased reverence for the Earth and all its life forms. The empathic resonance and synergistic strength of such a group allows the awesome power of the spirit realm to safely manifest into the finer substances of the physical plane with an even greater intensity than if it were at the behest of a single individual.

Several years after that uplifting experience with Lama Gangchen and the Blue Medicine Buddha, I was involved in a car accident. On the day after the collision I received a compassionate and skilled session of Bowen therapy to alleviate the pain of whiplash. As I lay on the bed I saw the Blue Buddha appear on my inner screen, and at that moment the pulsing shockwaves reverberating through my muscles ceased and the recovery to balance and well-being began.

* * *

The following procedure is recommended if you wish to develop your own ability to see the colour waves. It is advisable to follow this meditation during the seasons of spring and summer.

First, find and create your sheath of soul-quiet and anchor your grounding chord into the land. Secondly, free-fall into deep gratitude and appreciation until there is a warm ache around your heart. Thirdly, become aware of your pineal gland behind your third eye and greet your higher self. When you feel a stable connection with the divine, non-physical aspect of yourself, allow that part of you to greet the ruling nature spirit of your chosen location and wait in attentive responsiveness, remembering to breath rhythmically. If you are emanating the required resonance of sympathetic reverence, you may receive an immediate return greeting, but, if not, simply wait for a while and then ask if you may receive a response from the intelligence of the land.

When you eventually feel the heightened presence of the nature being of the location drawing towards you, ask if you may be allowed to see the supersensible colour haze. Soften your eyes into the all-encompassing 'plurality vision', instead of the normal focused singularity vision. If your mental, emotional and physical vehicle is resonating at an appropriate level of poise and attentive good will, you will begin to see expressions of colour over the land. These colours have a very different quality to the colours locked down into physical matter; they have a very specific iridescence. Many people see an iridescent mauve, lilac or yellow in these exchanges. A close analogy of this visual experience is to imagine a landscape scene on your computer screen. Then as you stare at the scene, some of the pixels cut out and a shimmering light begins to shine through where they had once been.

Don't be discouraged if you do not see the colour waves during your first attempts; it takes time to develop the visual acuity needed to accommodate or decode the high vibration of these colour waves. As always, be willing to 'fail' in the early stages, and remember that impatience will always close the window into the etheric realms. A regular meditative practice will mark a rhythm in the rotation of time, and this rhythm alone can strengthen your developing organs of seership -- regardless of whether you feel your meditation was successful or not. As you adapt to a rhythm of withdrawal and return – a withdrawal to the eternal and a return to the temporal – the desired results will eventually be forthcoming.

When you do begin to see the colour waves in nature, it is important to stay poised and breathe regularly. Do not try to grasp the experience and lock it down into the reasoning mind. Just hold back and allow the etheric expression to reveal itself and simply witness it while gently acknowledging your emotional state. You will probably feel a strong pull from the mental plane, so drop your attention down into your heart or solar plexus and gently witness the various sensations arising there. These sensations are the beginnings of a new language, which in time will become familiar and interpretable.

When the colour form has receded, stay in your breathing for a while before attempting to analyse what you have seen. The first experience of these colour waves is always a heart-warming and joyful revelation, a confirmation that you are truly on the right path. However, when you begin to experience these phenomena, it is of the utmost importance that you keep your own counsel and do not recount your experiences here, there and everywhere. You will lose considerable ground if you speak too soon. If you are working alone, it is advisable to keep your experiences to yourself for at least six months. If you are working in a group, then the need to keep your own counsel is not so critical. But if you are in any doubt about sharing your experiences with others, query this doubt in meditation. You will very quickly receive a 'yea' or 'nay' regarding the propriety of immediately sharing your insights with others.

Another essential step to remember is to *always* close an audience with the nature spirits and elementals with clear-cut intention and thanks. You could mark this closure with a phrase like: 'I give thanks at the altar of the threshold.' Also, if you have extended your protective sheath or sphere out into the landscape remember to draw it back into yourself. And finally, when you begin your journey home, remember to ground yourself fully in the physical world of humans. For example, when you get behind the wheel of your car say three times, 'I am driving the car,' or if you are walking home say to yourself, 'I am walking home in full awareness with my feet on the ground.' Focus yourself in present time and check that all your senses are awake and alert. To leave a doorway open across the threshold is both unwise and untidy, and at certain times it can also be unsafe.

Defence Against Psychic Attack

The cautionary note above leads us to the topic of psychic attack and the prevailing tendency to surround this subject with fantasy and glamour. There are of course adepts and groups who consciously exercise invasive techniques in order to influence people's decisions, and this includes the manipulative and aggressive techniques used in certain media practices and corporate advertising campaigns. However, as long as you remain attentive and aware of what you are doing, and you follow the steps of protection mentioned in the 'How to' section, you should remain relatively immune to such disruptive influences. The incidents loosely grouped under the title 'psychic attack' usually occur as a result of someone endeavouring to manipulate spiritual energies for their own gain, someone attempting to inhibit another person's freedom in order to force an outcome, or someone desperately seeking to appear different and special in some way in order to compensate for emotional insecurity. Such meddling nearly always backfires, because by its very nature it attracts the chaos and disruption of lower Devachan into the space-time reality of the one perpetrating the mischief in the first place.

The first line of defence against any form of psychic attack is to gain a basic understanding of the nature of the supersensible world. A strong connection with the inner guidance system of your higher self and a recognition of the effect your thi king 'life has on the elemental presence around you is also essential. In short, malevolent elementals are attracted to malevolent thinking, and they multiply around sustained negative intent. They are compelled to yield to whatever shade of morality they find before them. If you find yourself at the receiving end of negative intent, first ask yourself why you have attracted it, and where you have left yourself vulnerable. The next step is to take responsibility for your own protection by strengthening your sheath of soul-quiet, staying well grounded and deepening your connection with the intuitive intelligence of your higher self. By following these guidelines and remaining poised and centred, you will eventually tap into a source of helpful and insightful guidance. Whether this guidance surfaces from deep within yourself or it surfaces as an unmistakeable sign leading you to the wisdom and help of others, your task here is to abide by an unshakeable belief in your own innate ability to disarm and deflect such mischief. And of course, if you follow a religion, a heartfelt petition to the Divine in whatever form you understand it will always strengthen you in such a situation.

If we aspire to evolve into enlightened seers and mature stewards of this planet, we will have to learn new skills and become more self-sufficient. By committing unfailingly to a regular communion with the divine wisdom of the higher self within ourselves, we can go a long way towards achieving these aspirations.

The point of working with the elemental kingdom is first and foremost about developing our capacity to be of service to humanity and the Earth. It is about acknowledging and taking responsibility for the supersensible capacities within ourselves that are our divine birthright. We simply have to awaken these capacities and use them wisely, in order to cooperate successfully with the invisible kingdoms of the Earth. Building an effective protection around ourselves before interacting with these invisible kingdoms is a ritual of common sense and good manners, and in time it will become as familiar as putting on a seat-belt before taking a drive.

Authentic Experiences and Intense States of Awareness

The single most important thing to do when you begin to work with the elementals and nature spirits in your chosen location, is to send out the following message in strong, heartfelt imagery and tones:

'I BELIEVE IN YOU!'

By declaring this belief, you immediately sound a loud bell in the ether. The plurality of beings who inhabit the ether in your area will then be able to approach you through this open channel of belief. The responses will be many and varied, so it would be wise to expect the unexpected!

While the colour waves and whorls of light are the most widely reported visual phenomena in response to a greeting, there are, of course, many other forms of response from the elementals. So don't be disappointed, and don't be tempted into the drama of feeling you have failed if you do not immediately see these things. Be willing to 'fail'. Rudolf Steiner tells us that: 'The powers and faculties to be developed are, at the beginning, of a very delicate kind, and differ entirely from any ideas that may have been previously formed of them by the individual concerned.'[96] It is so easy to lose perseverance when we feel there is no tangible progress. Yet with every effort we make we strengthen these delicate organs of perception developing in our etheric body.

I remember one summer I was feeling particularly disheartened and disconsolate about my rate of progress. The responses from the elementals had been scant, short and fleeting for many months, and there had been long stretches of muteness between these responses. I had begun to believe that the nature spirit of 'my' hill had no interest in developing a line of communication with me any more.

Then one evening I pulled on my walking boots and set out in search of a glimpse of the new moon. As I leant against a gate and scanned the sky for a thin crescent of silver, I could hear the Welsh mare from the farm next door ambling across the field behind me. She found her way to me and put her head over my shoulder. As I stroked her warm velvety nose, she playfully nibbled and tugged at the wooden toggles of my duffel coat. Then suddenly we were both arrested by a very powerful presence. We both simultaneously switched into a heightened state of alertness. I was catapulted into that now familiar state of timelessness, and the mare instantly ceased playing, jerked up her head and pricked her ears forward. I could feel the cells of my body vibrating at an increased rate, and I experienced the environment around me through a new, heightened sensory awareness. The nature spirit of the area made its powerful presence felt. I experienced this being as benign yet grave, kind yet austere, and patient yet exhorting. Before my inner eye I was shown a wide tableau in which every prayer, every effort and every deed of good will I had directed to the elemental kingdom since I had moved onto the hill was recorded. Each prayer and deed was still resounding on, still living, still abiding, and still influencing the spin of the source field in its own particular way. The message conveyed to me by the nature spirit of the hill was simple: 'All you do in love is recorded here in the ether. We acknowledge you. Continue to work with us and tell others to do the same!'

The experience of seeming abandonment I had felt prior to this gracious exchange is an essential part of the course. The testimonials of saints, sages and seers throughout the ages have always shown that the nature spirits and angelic beings who are consciously petitioned to work with humanity have to test our mental-emotional strength and perseverance. Endlessly repeating exercises and regularly sending prayers and rituals into a seemingly mute landscape for months at a time are essential rites of passage on the road to a serious working relationship with the living intelligence of the Earth. The eventual reward is a warm, deep and powerful sense of kinship with the ancient spirits of the land, and a profound sense of usefulness and self-worth as one begins to acquire the 'Knowingness of the Earth'. To become a valuable messenger and a useful journeyman between the spiritual dimensions and the physical human world is vital work at this time in our evolution.

Each of us is constituted differently, and each of us has a unique set of references in our internal library. Our higher organs of perception will receive the responses from the elementals, and will interpret them through our own individual thinking-feeling apparatus in a way most suited to our life experience. For most of us, there is no exact way to translate into linear thinking the complex range of feelings we will experience during an early exchange with the nature spirits; therefore it is crucial to discipline the mind to stand back and allow the emerging feelings to swell and flow without hooking them into a premature mental storyline.

The key indications that you are experiencing an authentic interaction with the elemental world, are:

- You feel 'The Remembrance'.
- You feel a vibrational blending with your surroundings; you feel more porous.
- You feel a pure rush of warmth around your heart, a graceful knowingness untainted by sentimentality.
- You feel a heightened sensory awareness with your entire body.
- You sense activity in the corner of your eye.
- You may find your mouth beginning to water.
- You feel a tingling sensation, especially in your hands and/or in your upper jaw.
- You feel a sensation of time slowing down.
- You sense the colours in nature becoming more vibrant and mobile.
- You find yourself spontaneously bursting into laughter as you 'get it'. The acute pathos and the divine comedy of life join together to produce a tremendous burst of realization, which culminates in a roar of humorous recognition. The nature spirits have an exquisite sense of humour at times.
- You may feel an impulse to leave an offering – to make some sort of exchange – be it a song, a prayer, or an offering of food or drink. Such gestures are powerful signs to the nature spirits.
- An unexpected image or symbol may appear on the inner screen – allow it to be there without mental investigation for a while, then drop it down into the heart and solar plexus for a 'feeling analysis'. At a later point you may find that the image acts as a trigger or a clue to an important revelation about yourself or about the location you are working in. Deciphering symbols and their attendant feelings soon becomes a new form of language analysis in your everyday communications.
- You may tap into time-lines of the past. It is not unusual to encounter the events and ancestors of the past on the inner

screen when you begin to meditate in a specific location. If this happens, first ascertain if there is a symbol or message being offered to you, and if there is not, just give a nod of recognition and move on into the structure of the landscape.

In time you will experience a direct communion with the nature spirits. Human language is nearly always inadequate at describing these meetings, but one way of knowing your interaction is real and authentic is the sense of timelessness you find yourself in. This time-out-of-time timelessness is deeply poignant; the biography of the Earth can reveal itself in a large tableau and impress itself upon you, and once again, you can feel 'The Remembrance'. The transference of information you receive from nature's emissaries at these moments can often generate an almost intolerable ache, because the true scale of humanity's ingratitude and the ignorant maltreatment of the Earth is revealed through waves of emotion. In these moments, the 'sea of love', described by Dorothy Maclean, is tangible, and it can be both infinitely beautiful and implacably stern.

A deep and profound understanding of the interconnectedness of all life awakens in you, and you begin to comprehend how your identity transcends the boundary of skin to air and extends up into the stars. The meeting with the nature spirits in the sea of love cannot be hurried; impatience just delays it further. A dimensional doorway will only yield when you are deemed ready.

At some locations you may feel a wall of resistance. In such instances, you are being told that it is either the wrong time to interact or that you have not reached a level where you can assimilate and interact with the astral-etheric voltage of a place. Respect this denial until you are ready to be admitted.

It is well to remember that countless wars, battles and atrocities have occurred over the face of the Earth and that they can leave a fearsome residue in the energetic fields of a location. At a later point, when you have gained some experience and a certain proficiency in navigating the astral-etheric dimensions, you may join with others to clean up and transform the negative energies held at a specific location in your area. This is vital work and a worthy aspiration to have at this time in history. So much of the world's population, especially in the West, is unaware of the impact these pockets of supersensible stress can have on the plant, animal and human kingdoms. Often lasting for generations, we unwittingly add to their potency with our own unenlightened and impure thoughts, words and deeds. This particular spiritual knowledge highlights again the need for joyful rituals and celebrations to be observed around the seasonal phases of the year. When these gatherings are celebrated at wounded locations, both outside in nature and inside our community buildings, the sounds and sentiments of joyful celebration and deep gratitude will help to dismantle the energies of long-held memory. Such communal deeds of joy reverberate through the old, negative thought forms held in the ether, and release the long-suffering elementals imprisoned by past deeds of human error.

> We who give the elementals so many hard tasks can contribute greatly to their lives if we share in the right way in the breathing of the Earth, by celebrating the festivals of the year ... When the elementals see this coming about, they can recognise with joy that men are beginning to share in some of their tasks and do not only hinder them. And the creative works of men will take their harmonious place among all living things on Earth.[97]
>
> Adam Bittleston

8

Helping the Elementals at Home and at Work

In this chapter we look at the following themes: how to help the elementals in our immediate environment; clearing and enhancing the supersensible atmosphere of our communal spaces with focused thoughts, words and deeds; the healing power of biodynamic agriculture; protecting ourselves in an urban environment.

Whether you live in the country or in a city, you can build a meaningful relationship with the elementals in your home and at your place of work. Here are some suggestions for enhancing the atmosphere in your living space:

1) Firstly, ensure that there is good ventilation throughout your home and allow new air elementals into your rooms on a daily basis. Secondly, choose some high-quality sacred music to clear any dense or nervous energy from your living space. The sounds of Tibetan singing bowls, Gregorian chants and overtoning can all make a significant difference to the atmosphere of your home. The music of Bach and Mozart, as we have already learnt, has a beneficial effect on the structure of water and will have a similar balancing effect on the air. The sound of sacred hymns, chants, bhajans and prayers transforms that which lives impure in ourselves and our surroundings. This is why cathedrals, temples and mosques maintain such a rarefied and sacred atmosphere; they are regularly absorbing the sound-waves of human voices raised in praise.

Even if the music suggested above is not to your taste, simply leave it playing in your home while you are out. If you do this for several days in a row, you will notice a subtle difference in the atmosphere of your surroundings. The air spirits are the carriers of speech and tone through the element of air, and they will be reinvigorated by such pure tones. Live music is, of course, the most effective, but it is not always possible or practical in the home and office environment. Try using flower essence sprays after heated discussions and angry exchanges. The undines and sylphs in the spray have a balancing effect on the fire spirits of the agitated thought forms. In extreme cases, try smudging the room — this is a Native American practice of burning dried sage leaves. The strong smelling smoke acts as a rigorous cleansing agent in the astral-etheric body of a human being as well as the astral-etheric field of a location.

2) Endeavour to use environmentally friendly cleaning products. If there is a task that appears to need a more rugged substance, inform the elementals of what you are about to do before commencing. You do this by briefly running a 'mental movie' of what you are about to do, and directing it towards the area in which you are about to work. This kind of visual precursor can be used in many situations. For example, if you wish to mow your lawn, before you begin either walk over the grass or stand close to the lawn and project a strong image of what you are about to do over the entire area. There are many insects and small amphibians who live amongst the grasses and they have a direct connection with the elemental kingdom.

It is the persistent, mindless disregard for the consequences of our actions that redounds so heavily on the elemental world. Therefore by choosing to consciously interact with the elemental beings in our home and immediate environment we can go some way towards mitigating the damage we may occasionally do by using a harsh cleaning product or enacting a thoughtless deed. The elementals, and especially the gnomes, are here to maintain a robust cycle of materialization on the physical plane — it is their divine purpose to do so. There is no need to become mawkish or over-sentimental when using the visual precursor. It is simply a courteous practice to cultivate on the path towards a full co-creative partnership with the elemental kingdom.

3) Every time you turn on a tap, acknowledge and give thanks to the undines.

4) Each time you light a candle, honour and give thanks to the fire spirits. And when you are ready to snuff out the flame, try using the following phrase: 'This goes out but not the Sun, I do not end what has begun.' Send the fire forward, respect the flame.

5) Introduce some rocks, stones and crystals into your home and place them on the window sill. By contemplating a particularly fine slice of granite, agate or serpentine, or by studying the dynamic angles of a quartz crystal you will put yourself back in touch with the work wrought during Earth's long history and the forces of Creation. Rocks and crystals will be a daily reminder that the mineral realm is embedded with a subtle consciousness of its own.

Remember to cleanse and recharge your rocks and crystals regularly. This can be done by placing them in a sunny spot on the bare earth or putting them against a tree trunk. (It is advisable to keep delicately coloured crystals like amethyst and fluorite out of strong sunlight, as the colour will begin to fade after a while.) You can also cleanse and recharge your rocks and crystals with the energy of running water, by placing them in a stream, holding them under the tap or leaving them out in the rain.

6) Nurture the plants in your home.

7) Say grace and give thanks to the elementals of your food before you eat.

8) Pay attention to the food you eat. The SAD diet, or Standard American Diet of refined sugars and flours, interferes with our ability to access higher levels of consciousness and it calcifies the pineal gland. By choosing organic and biodynamic produce, both the elementals in the food and the elementals in our physical organs can interact and combine to enhance our intuitive ability as well as our physical health.

9) In the winter months make a conscious effort to let the Sun's rays into your eyes, taking care not to strain them. Breathe in the rays and imagine them beaming into your pineal gland, filling the

cranium and travelling down your spine. The Sun is an exalted sentient Being in our solar system, and the fire spirits on its rays will enter us in a beneficial way if we acknowledge and appreciate them.

10) Practise listening using your entire body. Listening is a form of respectful devotion.

11) Whenever possible, try to walk barefoot on the earth, or endeavour to wear shoes without rubber soles when you can. Rubber soles inhibit the energy of the Earth from entering our feet. Many of us work in an office environment and only experience brief periods of communion with the natural world, especially during the winter months, and as such we become disconnected from the Earth. We build up a lot of static electricity around our bodies and this can put a strain on the immune system. By walking barefoot or wearing light leather-soled shoes, we can ground this static electricity and receive instead the health-bearing negatively charged ions emanating from the Earth. Also, after a long car or plane journey, try leaning down and touching the Earth; this will help to ground the build-up of static electricity. This gesture, of course, is also a way of greeting the elementals of a new location.

12) While walking the land, remember to walk with your eyes raised to the horizon ahead of you, rather than always focusing on the ground. This helps to develop the all-inclusive, or plurality, vision required for supersensible seership.

13) If you have a garden, try to use biodynamic preparations[98] on your plants and soil. By doing so, you fertilize, enliven and harmonize the dynamic forces working in the ether, and you aid the elementals in their tasks.

In 1924, Rudolf Steiner introduced the principles of biodynamic gardening and farming in a series of lectures entitled the *Agriculture Course*. He presented this series in response to a plea for help from a group of farmers and landowners who had become greatly concerned by the increase in animal diseases and soil deterioration following the rise of industrial farming after the First World War. At the core of the *Agriculture Course* is the recognition that the Earth is a self-regulating, multidimensional ecosystem, and that the ecology of the farm-organism is intimately related to the movements of the entire cosmos. The biodynamic principles incorporate an understanding of the dynamic and responsive quality of the astral-etheric forces in nature. They also emphasize the importance of the human being at the centre of the organism, whether that organism be a thousand-acre vineyard or a small town garden.

A combination of supersensible insight and enhanced observation allows the biodynamic grower to begin to operate across multiple levels of reality and, at a later point, to intervene in the predetermined processes of nature in a sensitive, conscious and life-enhancing way. The farm or garden then develops into a responsive extension of the grower's own body, while at the same time stimulating a new multi-sensory will activity. 'In biodynamic farming we can have the inner certainty that the deeper we enter into spiritual insight, the more we are serving an evolutionary process.'[99]

The mindless, destructive programme of mega-scale industrial farming, GMO seed manipulation and heavy use of harsh fertilizers has left large areas of arable land on the planet exhausted, desensitized and wounded. Yet in the wisdom and application of biodynamics we have an effective medicine and methodology which has proved, and is still proving, to be a powerful healer of the land. The key preparations at the centre of the biodynamic method of agriculture are the horn manure and horn silica spray preparations. They are made from specially fermented cow dung (preparation 500) and finely ground quartz crystal (preparation 501), which have been packed into cow horns and buried under the soil for several months. They draw in and harness the vital, dynamic forces of the Earth, as she breathes the elementals into herself in the winter and then releases them back into the atmosphere during the summer. Rhythm is the great carrier of life! Huge amounts of energy are conserved in the contraction of the winter months, followed by a great expansion and release during the summer exhalation. These potent preparations are then sprinkled into water and dynamized — a process by which water is vigorously stirred in one direction until a substantial vortex is formed in the bucket or barrel. Throughout the process of dynamizing, it is the human being who wields the spiral and becomes the conscious creator, and after the water has been stirred in alternating directions for an hour the potent, enlivened liquid is then sprayed onto the land.

The archetypal image of the vortex echoes throughout Creation: it expresses itself in the vast spiral of the galactic superwave emanating from the centre of the Milky Way, and it also leaves its delicate trace in the perfectly formed shell of a snail.

Not only do the preparations and methods used in biodynamic agriculture increase the vitality of the soil, regulate imbalances, encourage root growth and enhance flavour and nutrition, they also have a positive effect on levels of radiation in the soil — as shown by readings taken on biodynamically farmed land around Chernobyl. The wisdom contained in the *Agriculture Course* is a healing medicine for the whole multi-dimensional organism of the planet, and it gives humanity an opportunity to take an active role in endowing nature with evolutionary processes.

Further investigation into the beneficial methods and effects of biodynamics is highly recommended.[100]

* * *

When you honour and work with the elementals on the land, in your home and in your body they will return your greeting and respect in many health-bearing ways. After a while, the combined sensory mechanism of your heart, mind and solar plexus will pick up the fine nuances emanating from the nature spirits and elementals in your environment, and you will begin to intuit wise ways and choices with even more speed and accuracy.

However, there can be a downside to this sensitivity in the early stages of supersensible work. If you live in an area of environmental tension, you may tap into the astral-etheric stress of the location in a way which is overwhelming on occasions. To guard against this, remember to reinforce your 'sheath of soul-quiet' and focus on your own designated mini-sphere. You can always expand your own field outwards when you are in the familiar territory of your home or when you become more experienced in this work. If you live in a city, it is advisable to join a group of like-minded souls on the same path – this creates a stronger protective shield in the first stages of seership. We are not here to save the entire solar system single-handed! We are here to heal and transform our own astral-etheric body, and to extend this will for healing out into our locality. By focusing on this vital personal task, we are positively affecting the whole and contributing to the momentum of planetary healing.

For those who live in a city or an area of astral-etheric tension, a meditation by Rudolf Steiner can be used as an extra protective layer against invasive thought forms in the construction of the 'sheath of soul-quiet'. It runs as follows:

> The blue outer sheath of my aura thickens
> It surrounds me with an impenetrable vessel (skin)
> Against all impure, unpurified thoughts and sensations
> Only divine wisdom enters it.[101]

And below is an adaptation from the original:

> Beautiful blue bell, be around me
> May the outer sheath of my aura grow dense
> That I become an impenetrable vessel
> Against all impure, unpurified thoughts, feelings and sensations
> And I open only to divine wisdom

Before using this phrase, ensure that you feel firmly grounded, by mentally dropping your anchor into the earth, or by sitting with your back against a tree, a wall or a pillar. This grounding con-nection ensures that any trapped negativity can be directed down into the earth.

Endeavour to remember that all thoughts and words create form on a subtle level. Therefore in order to create an effective shield speak out clearly with authority, and make sure you truly envision the protective sheath around you. Good mental, verbal and physical preparation is an essential practice before placing yourself in an open and receptive state. It is considered good spiritual housework and, in time, it will become as familiar as putting on your favourite coat.

9

A New Human Being and a New Earth

In the final chapter we look at the battle being fought for the human soul and psyche, in both the material and spiritual realms. We also consider the healing power of forgiveness.

The astral body of both the Earth and the individual human being is an engine room of transformation at this time in history. It is the battlefield on which the transformative processes are taking place. The emotional wave of the Earth's astral body pulses around the planet like a jet stream and we are either contributing or responding to it with the waves of antipathy and sympathy we emit and receive. This astral field is also home to the vast human thought forms, holding many of us in their grip. The emotional feedback from military conflict, fundamentalist religion, manipulative media and corporate malpractice hover over us like menacing storm clouds. Their ever more sophisticated modes of incursion into our daily lives will only increase, until we wake up to the nature and power of our own subtle, supersensible bodies. There is a war of frequency playing out in these invisible realms and the treasure being fought over is the human soul. Yet, we have never been powerless, and every time we witness and resolve an agitating wave of fear, anger or vengeance within ourselves we are contributing to the purification of this planetary astral-emotional wave.

The Earth is our greater body and the collective mass of human thought and emotion impacts the working balance of our planet's astral and etheric field; this in turn influences the elementals in the creation of weather and seismic activity. The increasingly severe weather anomalies we are experiencing are an outward expression of humanity's accumulated stress and dilemma, meeting the climate change of the entire solar system. Our mission today is to know that everything is primed with life and consciousness, everything is interconnected and everyone is ultimately related. Our highly receptive friends the nature spirits and elementals of earth, who exist in a state of eternal metamorphosis and sensitive change-ability, are evolving alongside us in a dimension that is only a thought-step and an emotion away. It is time to reach out to them, to learn from them and to become responsible, joyful stewards of the natural world with them.

The journey starts with a commitment to an open mind, it develops into a highway of anticipation, wonder and revelation, and then it eventually brings us out onto a plateau of deep love and respect. For too long humanity has believed in its right of dominion over the natural world. Today there is a new Earth and a new radiance being born through us, and in the words of that great visionary Eckhart Tolle, humanity is faced with a stark choice: 'Evolve or Die'.[102] We cannot hire someone to find enlightenment for us, we cannot blackmail someone into giving it to us, and in the end there will be nowhere left to hide from the necessity of self-realization. We must face our darkest shadows with courage and accountability if we are to chose the light-filled, upward path of evolution, because there is no place for the illusionist, the environmental thief or the ruthlessly self-centred in the new world we are creating. Their destiny lies on the ever-hardening path of materialism with its diminishing resources, endless legislation and restricted awareness, and at some point in the millennia to come the drawbridge between the upward and downward path will be pulled up. Those who have consistently served the gods of unremitting materialism will lose their chance to evolve into the next stage of human evolution.

A new species of human being is emerging and the old ways will no longer serve us. The new path of service is one where we serve the greater whole, and those who cannot bear the light of the new consciousness will incarnate elsewhere. Humanity as a species will begin to split.

For those who are awake and aware, the pathway to a New Earth beckons. And if we were to narrow the 'New Earth Preparatory Manual' down to three essential directives they would run as follows:

(i) Acknowledge, honour and work with the background living presence within nature wherever, whenever and however you can.

(ii) Witness your thinking and pivot it into positive creativity whenever and however you can.

(iii) Become an adept of forgiveness until there is nothing left to forgive.

The first two are graspable, and suitably elastic and responsive to the growing levels of consciousness in an awakening individual, but even some of the most experienced students on the path of spiritual enlightenment baulk at commencing a true and lasting act of forgiveness. Forgiveness requires a level of personal strength and willpower that many people just cannot find within themselves. It is almost a taboo subject; it can whip up a blizzard of cold fury, contempt and excuses within seconds, followed later by a milder front of stubborn resistance and justification. Yet, this raw, exposed frontier of forgiveness is one we must endeavour to reach. There is no way around the sixth petition of 'forgiving the trespass' – it is implacable – and in our deepest heart we know there will always be a 'ring-pass-not' waiting for us until we do forgive.

However, there are ways and means of crossing this frontier. In the exquisite book *Prayers of the Cosmos*, mentioned in Chapter 2, author Neil Douglas-Klotz has translated the original Aramaic text of the Lord's Prayer. These translations inject a new, living, breathing presence into the sixth petition, and they transcend individual religious doctrine. They ignite a new understanding of this ancient and persistent dilemma, and they offer a new set of coordinates with which to navigate through the chaotic emotions of forgiveness.

'Loose the cords of mistakes binding us, as we release the strands
we hold of other's guilt'

'Forgive our hidden past, the secret shames, as we constantly
forgive what others hide'

'Erase the inner marks our failures make, just as we scrub our
hearts of others' faults'

'Untangle the knots within, so that we can mend our hearts'
simple ties to others'[103]

Contemplating the reasons for a traumatic event in our life can
often trigger a relentless cycle of revenge and blame, and if we allow
this cycle to continue unchecked it will ultimately rob us of valuable
life energy. There are many ways to break such a cycle. They range
from a physical practice like EFT (Emotional Freedom Technique),
which involves regularly tapping key meridian points on the body
in order to release trauma stored in the physical and etheric bodies,
to the more mental-emotional based techniques, which precipitate a
loosening of the trauma by re-contextualizing it with the witnessing
consciousness. In her excellent book *Loving What Is*, mentioned
earlier in Chapter 6, author Byron Katie offers an effective strategy
for out-smarting and dismantling the debilitating waves of enmity
that circulate through a traumatized human mind. She uses a set of
razor-sharp questions to disarm every slight, crime or abuse
experienced in the past. This prevents the negative memories from
appropriating our thinking life in the present; she calls this process
'The Work.'[104] These simple, but brilliantly crafted questions impel
us to revisit the 'crime-scene' with a new heightened awareness, and
by doing so we can get a clearer understanding of how and why the
disturbing event happened in the first place. The greatest gift these
questions bring is the realization that our own individual evolutionary path will only ever hover in stubborn stasis until we give up
the grudge.

But we are human! And the collective strength of our emotions is
the most powerful force on the planet. Our antipathies can

imprison us for an entire lifetime and can send us over the edge of reason, as the seemingly never-ending wars around the world testify. For some an act of forgiveness takes decades of perseverance. But for others it takes place only at the threshold of death, because at this point some intimation of the burdensome, transmigratory nature of vengeance begins to dawn upon us. We will all line up with the necessity of forgiveness at some point in our lives, and deep within our hearts we know it is a task that cannot be forever postponed.

In his moving and powerful book entitled *The Occult Significance of Forgiveness*, Sergei. O. Prokofieff reveals how 'forgiving the trespass' manifests a shimmering sphere of potential in the supersensible world. He writes: 'As [man] beholds his past earthly life in the Akashic Record, he perceives in place of every act of forgiveness that he has accomplished on the earth what could be described as the emergence of a free "space", which . . . is gradually filled with the substance of Christ.'[105] Whatever name represents this divine substance for you, be it the love of Christ, the mercy of Allah, the light of the Siddhi or the wisdom of Great Spirit, this gracious substance is waiting to fill the space your deeds of forgiveness create. Forgiveness collapses time and it releases waves of precious elementals back into the flow of life.

As we create these free spaces, they begin to undermine and deconstruct the huge negative thought-forms brooding over humanity and the Earth. By detaching ourselves from the grip of judgement and vengeance, and by consciously spiralling our thinking into higher octaves of creativity, we not only lighten our individual and collective load but also free vast numbers of elemental beings from their imprisonment in these forms. Every time we achieve an act of forgiveness or reach out with love and respect to the spirit in nature, we are moulding the supersensible waveform with human grace. The resulting shape and hue of its sensible particle will be the ultimate testimony of our prowess as enlightened co-creators of the Earth.

There are, of course, those who would rather not know about the nature spirits and elementals, because the personal responsibility that goes with such knowledge is too threatening for the autonomy of the human ego. To vociferously deny the supersensible world and its inhabitants, showering derision over those who speak of them, seems far easier than facing up to the reality that there is no such thing as a private thought or a privileged point of observation.

Yet somewhere between the rigid atheists, inflexible reductionists and scornful sceptics, who grind and lock down every luminous expression of nature into weights, measures and labels ... and the ranting soothsayers, compulsive sensationalists and determined escapists, who regularly sabotage their own fragile faculties of supersensible perception with excessive drama and emotion – somewhere between these two extremes lies an old and well-formed path, with mottled beams lighting the way. It is a path that leads to a timeless place of knowingness, where weights, measures and matter dance effortlessly with ether, spirit and divinity. Once you have drawn from the wisdom of this place and felt the rush of remembrance, there is no turning back; you have no choice but to see more, feel more and be more. The ancient sacred gift of seership, which was once a fully apparent gift in humanity, is returning – but it will only come to flower in those who choose to awaken from the slumber of forgetfulness.

* * *

I wish you well on your path. May the fire spirits inspire you and The Remembrance grow within you.

Notes

1. Adam Bittleston, *Counselling and Spiritual Development*, Floris Books, Edinburgh 1988, p. 154.
2. Mission statement by William Tiller — for further information visit www.tiller.org
3. Project Camelot interview, Ecuador, February 2009. http://projectcamelot.org/brian_o_leary.html
4. Reciprocal space is defined as momentum space, in contrast to real space or direct space.
5. Quantum coherence refers to circumstances when large numbers of particles can collectively cooperate in a single quantum state.
6. Mae-Wan Ho, Physicist, 'Quantum Coherence and Conscious Experience'. The full article can be found at the Institute of Science and Society website, www.i-sis.org.uk
7. Philippians 4:7.
8. *Bhagavad Gita, the Book of Devotion*, edited by William Q. Judge, Kessinger Publishing, Whitefish, MT, 2004, p. 36.
9. Rudolf Steiner, *Correspondence and Documents 1901–1925*, SteinerBooks, Great Barrington, MA, 1988, p. 14.
10. Cognitive process.
11. James Schomburg, *Chronicles of Beyond, Book 1*, Tate Publishing, London 2009, p. 279.
12. Further information on the programmable wave structure of DNA can be found in Chapters 9 and 10 of *The Source Field Investigations* by David Wilcock, Penguin, New York 2011.
13. Dr Paul LaViolette is a solar energy consultant for the United Nations and president of the Starburst Foundation.
14. The word coherent in this context means 'highly structured', like a laser beam.
15. Further information on the principles of torsion, and links to the replicated experiments carried out by Nikolai Kozyrev and other members of the Russian scientific community, can be found at divinecosmos.com on the following Link http://divinecosmos.com/start-here/books-free-online/20 -the-divine-cosmos/95-the-divine-cosmos-chapter-01-the-breakthroughs-of-dr-na-kozyrev

16. For further information on the work of Nikolai Kozyrev, including information on time-flow detection, follow the astrophysical observations section of *The Source Field Investigations* by David Wilcock, and also see his extended article on Kozyrev entitled 'Kozyrev: Aether, Time and Torsion' at www.divinecosmos.com. 'The Nature of Torsion and the Tiller Model of Psychoenergetic Science' at www.tillerfoundation.com provides further information on torsion field physics.

17. For the full article on torsion fields and time detection by Yuri Nachalov, go to http://amasci.com/freenrg/tors/tors3.html

18. The study of visible sound and vibration.

19. Rudolf Steiner, *The Inner Nature of Music and the Experience of Tone*, Anthroposophic Press, 1983. Or find on http://wn.rsarchive.org/Lectures/InNatMusic/19221202p01.html

20. *Secret Life of Chaos* was first broadcast on BBC Four in January 2010.

21. A unified consciousness of a specific group of beings.

22. By permission from the R.J. Stewart Inner Temple Discussion List at yahoo.com

23. Neil Douglas-Klotz, *Prayers of the Cosmos: Meditations on the Aramaic Words of Jesus*, HarperCollins, San Francisco 1990, p. 12.

24. Excerpt from the 2010 Prophet Conference — for the full article visit http://www.greatmystery.org/nl/vancouver2012daniel.html

25. Michael Anthony Corey, *The God Hypothesis* Rowman & Littlefield, Lanham, MD, 2007, p. 257.

26. Excerpt from the 2010 Project Camelot Interview with Graham Hancock, http://www.youtube.com/watch?v=UkCnE8YdFP0

27. For a short overview of biodynamic agriculture go to p. 145.

28. Nicolas Joly, *Wine from Sky to Earth*, Acres Publishing, Austen, TX, 1999, p. 149.

29. Rupert Sheldrake, *The Science Delusion: Freeing the Spirit of Enquiry*, Coronet, London 2012, introductory pages. Or find on http://ww.cygnus-books.co.uk/magazine/2011/12/freeing-the-spirit-of-enquiry/

30. Rudolf Steiner, *Harmony of the Creative Word*, Rudolf Steiner Press, 2001.

31. A supersensible dimension, or sphere of consciousness, wherein the entire history of the Earth and humanity is recorded.

32. Excerpt from 'Science and Nonduality' DVD, Volume Two. For further information visit www.scienceandnonduality.com

33. For further information on sub-quantum kinetics, visit http://www.etheric.com/LaVioletteBooks/ether.html

34. Dorothy Maclean, *Kingdoms in Co-creation, Deva Messages*, Findhorn Foundation Tape Series, Lorian, 1979. The Lorian Association, PO Box 1368, Issaquah, WA 98027.

35. Psychoenergetics is the term used by Dr William Tiller for investigating the effects of human intention on both the properties of materials (inorganic and organic, non-living and living) and on what we call physical reality.

36. For more information about 'The Intention Experiment' visit www.intentionexperiment911.com/Intention.aspx

37. Dennis Klocek, *Weather and Cosmos*, Rudolf Steiner College, 1991, p. 90.

38. Dennis Klocek, *Climate: Soul of the Earth*, Lindisfarne Books, 2010, introduction p. xvi.

39. Nicolas Joly, *Wine from Sky to Earth*, Acres Publishing, 1999, p. 10.

40. For further information, see the article entitled 'The Signatures of the Divine' at http://www.amitgoswami.org

41. Rudolf Steiner, *World Ether, Elemental Beings, Kingdoms of Nature*, extracts compiled and annotated by Ernst Hagemann, Mercury Press, 2008, p. 25.

42. Rudolf Steiner, *Nature Spirits*, Rudolf Steiner Press, 2001, p. 118.

43. Rudolf Steiner, *World Ether, Elemental Beings, Kingdoms of Nature*, extracts compiled and annotated by Ernst Hagemann, Mercury Press, 2008, p. 23.

44. Ibid., p. 25.

45. William Tiller, www.tiller.org

46. Manfred Klett, *Principles of Biodynamic Spray and Compost Preparation*, Floris Books, Edinburgh 2006, p. 38.

47. Rudolf Steiner, *The Apocalypse of St John*, Anthroposophical Publishing Company, 1958 revised edition, p. 142.

48. René Querido, *The Golden Age of Chartres*, Floris Books, Edinburgh 1987, p. 49–50.

49. Nicolas Joly, *Wine from Sky to Earth*, Acres Publishing, Austen, TX, 1999, p. 119.

50. Rudolf Steiner, *World Ether, Elemental Beings, Kingdoms of Nature*, extracts compiled and annotated by Ernst Hagemann, Mercury Press, 2008, p. 28.

51. Ibid., p. 27.

52. Excerpt from the Living Water Flowforms website by Phil Sedgman, www.livingwaterflowforms.com

53. Lemniscate Flowforms are cascades of water flowing around a figure-of-eight curve. This movement aids the re-oxygenation of water and restores it to a purer state. For more information visit www.livingwaterflowforms.com and www.flowform.net

54. Verena Stael von Holstein, *Nature Spirits and What They Say*, Floris Books, Edinburgh 2004, p. 57.

55. Masaru Emoto, *The Healing Power of Water*, Hay House Publishing, Carls-bad,CA, 2007.

56. Dennis Klocek, *Climate: Soul of the Earth*, Lindisfarne Books, 2010, introduction page xvii.

57. Rudolf Steiner, *Nature Spirits*, Rudolf Steiner Press, 2001, p. 124.

58. Ernst Hagemann, *World Ether, Elemental Beings, Kingdoms of Nature*, Mercury Press, 2008, p. 29.

59. Founding Member of the International Consciousness Research Laboratory (ICRL) at Princeton University.

60. For further information on Nikolai Kozyrev's experimentation with time-flow detectors, and a description of the detectors themselves, see 'The Gravity of the Source Field' chapter in *The Source Field Investigations* by David Wilcock, Penguin, 2011.

61. For further information on the properties of time, the following titles are recommended: *On the possibility of experimental investigation of the properties of time* (English) by Professor N.A. Kozyrev, and *Thermodynamics of Real Processes* (Russian) by Professor A.I. Veinik.

62. Verena Stael von Holstein, *Nature Spirits and What They Say*, Floris Books, Edinburgh 2004, p. 70.

63. Rudolf Steiner, *St. John's: An Introductory Reader*, compiled with introduction by Matthew Barton, Rudolf Steiner Press, 2007, p. 12.

64. Excerpt from the Blooming Humans website, by Stacey Robyn www.bloominghumans.com

65. Rudolf Steiner, *Nature Spirits*, Rudolf Steiner Press, 2001, p. 49.

66. Ibid., p. 51.

67. Ernst Hagemann, *World Ether, Elemental Beings, Kingdoms of Nature*, Mercury Press, 2008, p. 31.

68. Rudolf Steiner, *Nature Spirits*, Rudolf Steiner Press, 2001, p. 127.

69. Ibid., p. 128.

70. *Forbidden Knowledge: The Secret of Creation*, video by Michael C. Markosky, http://www.youtube.com/watch?v=B6DplmnwEFA

71. Rudolf Steiner, *Harmony of the Creative Word*, Rudolf Steiner Press, 2001, p. 134.

72. Ernst Hagemann, *World Ether, Elemental Beings, Kingdoms of Nature*, Mercury Press, 2008, p. 33.

73. Bryan Hubbard, *Time Light*, New Age Publishing, London 2011.

74. A famous mountain in west Wales meaning 'Chair of Idris', referring to the giant warrior poet of Welsh legend.

75. Rudolf Steiner, *The Archangel Michael: His Mission and Ours*, selected lectures and writings, Rudolf Steiner Press, 1984, p. 287.

76. Rudolf Steiner, *The Apocalypse of St John*, Anthroposophical Publishing Company, 1958 revised edition, p. 157.

77. John O'Donohue, *Anam Cara*, Bantam Books, London 1999, p. 79.

78. For further information about the effects of meditation on the structure of the brain, visit the Massachusetts General Hospital (MGH) report on the Science Daily Website at
www.sciencedaily.com/releases/2011/01/110121144007.htm

79. Excerpt from the 2011 Fairness Campaign Summit
http://www.purposebalancelife.com/the-fairness-campaign-summit.html

80. Byron Katie, *Loving What Is*, Rider Books, London 2008, p. 179.

81. Dorothy Maclean, *Kingdoms in Co-creation, Deva Messages*, Findhorn Foundation Tape Series, Lorian, 1979, The Lorian Association, PO Box 1368, Issaquah, WA 98027.

82. Rudolf Steiner, *Nature Spirits*, Rudolf Steiner Press, 2001, p. 180.

83. Friedrich Rittelmeyer, *Meditation: Guidance of the Inner Life*, Floris Books, Edinburgh 1987.

84. Isha Judd, *Why Walk When You Can Fly?* New World Library, Novato 2008, p. 78.

85. Rudolf Steiner, *Six Steps in Self-Development. The Supplementary Exercises*, a collection compiled by Ates Baydur, Rudolf Steiner Press, Sussex, 2010.

86. *Complete Novels of Jane Austen*, Wordsworth Editions, 2007, p. 1037.

87. Rudolf Steiner mediated a new form of the Christian sacraments, and the new form of communion service is called 'The Act of Consecration of Man'. For further details about this service, please read an introduction to the Christian Community by Michael Tapp at http://antroposofi.org/ks/michaeltapp.htm or visit http://www.thechristiancommunity.co.uk

88. This booklet can be purchased from the Biodynamic Association at www.biodynamic.org.uk

89. For more information on the courses held at Hawkwood College visit www.hawkwoodcollege.co.uk

90. This small crystalline gland in the centre of the head has long been seen as the receptor, or point of interface, with the spiritual dimensions.

91. Rudolf Steiner, *Nature Spirits*, Rudolf Steiner Press, 2001, p. 24.

92. Ibid. pp. 173–50.

93. Marko Pogacnik, *Nature Spirits and Elemental Beings*, Findhorn Press, 2009, p. 62.

94. Ibid., p. 72.

95. Dorothy Maclean, *Kingdoms in Co-creation, Deva Messages*, Findhorn Foundation Tape Series, Lorian, 1979. The Lorian Association, PO Box 1368, Issaquah, WA 98027.

96. Rudolf Steiner, *Knowledge of the Higher Worlds*, Rudolf Steiner Press, 2009, p. 61.

97. Adam Bittleston, *Counselling and Spiritual Development*, Floris Books, Edinburgh 1988, p. 151.

98. For further information on the biodynamic preparations please visit www.biodynamic.org.uk

99. Manfred Klett, *Principles of Biodynamic Preparations*, Floris Books, 2006, p. 41.

100. Visit www.biodynamic.org.uk and www.biodynamics.com for further information.

101. Rudolf Steiner, *Start Now! Meditation Instructions, Meditations Prayers and Verses*, SteinerBooks, p. 176.

102. Eckhart Tolle, *A New Earth*, Penguin Books, London 2005, p. 21.

103. Neil Douglas-Klotz, *Prayers of the Cosmos: Meditations on the Aramaic Words of Jesus*, HarperCollins, San Francisco 1990, p. 30.

104. A visit to Byron Katie's website is recommended in order to see videos of 'The Work' in practice. www.thework.com

105. Sergei O. Prokofieff, *The Occult Significance of Forgiveness*, Temple Lodge Publishing, 2004, p. 97.

Recommended Reading

Rudolf Steiner, *Harmony of the Creative Word*, Rudolf Steiner Press, 2001

Rudolf Steiner, *Knowledge of the Higher Worlds*, Rudolf Steiner Press, 2009

Dorian Schmidt, *Observations in the Field of Formative Forces in Nature*. Available from the BDAA www.biodynamic.org.uk

David Wilcock, *The Source Field Investigations*, Penguin, New York 2011

Dennis Klocek, *Weather and Cosmos*, Rudolf Steiner College, 1991

Dennis Klocek, *Climate: Soul of the Earth*, Lindisfarne Books, 2010

Dennis Klocek, *The Seer's Handbook: A Guide to Higher Perception*, SteinerBooks, Great Barrington, MA, 2005

Nan Moss with David Corbin, *Weather Shamanism*, Bear & Company, Rochester, VT, 2008

Neil Douglas-Klotz, *Prayers of the Cosmos: Meditations on the Aramaic Words of Jesus*, HarperCollins, San Francisco 1990

Nicolas Joly, *What is Biodynamic Wine?*, Clairview Books, Sussex 2007

Byron Katie, with Stephen Mitchell, *Loving What Is: Four Questions That Can Change Your Life*, Harmony Books, New York 2002

Masaru Emoto, *The Hidden Messages in Water*, Hay House Publishing, Carlsbad, CA, 2007